Artificial Intelligence in the Behavioral Health PROFESSIONS

Ethical and Risk Management Issues

FREDERIC G. REAMER

NASW PRESS

National Association of Social Workers
Washington, DC

Cheryl Y. Mayberry Bradley, *Publisher*
Rachel Meyers, *Acquisitions Editor*
Julie Gutin, *Project Manager*

First impression: March 2025

Library of Congress Cataloging-in-Publication Data

Names: Reamer, Frederic G., 1953– author

Title: Artificial intelligence in the behavioral health professions : ethical and risk management issues / Frederic G. Reamer.

Description: Washington, DC : NASW Press, [2025] | Includes bibliographical references and index. | Summary: "The use of artificial intelligence (AI) is growing in the field of behavioral health in clinical, administrative, advocacy, policy, and educational settings. With that growth come ethical and risk management challenges. Through real-world examples and dozens of case studies, this concise guide provides insights into the ways in which behavioral health professionals are using AI, the ethical and risk management issues associated with practitioners' use of AI, protocols for ethical use of AI, and risk management strategies that will protect clients and practitioners alike"—Provided by publisher.

Identifiers: LCCN 2024061961 (print) | LCCN 2024061962 (ebook) | ISBN 9780871016270 paperback | ISBN 9780871016287 ebook

Subjects: LCSH: Social service—Technological innovations | Mental health services—Technological innovations | Artificial intelligence—Moral and ethical aspects

Classification: LCC HV40 .R3439 2025 (print) | LCC HV40 (ebook) | DDC 362.20285—dc23/eng/20250224

LC record available at https://lccn.loc.gov/2024061961

LC ebook record available at https://lccn.loc.gov/2024061962

Printed in the United States of America

For Deborah, Emma, Leah, Chris, and Jackson

Table of Contents

1

Artificial Intelligence in the Behavioral Health Professions: An Overview

ARTIFICIAL INTELLIGENCE (AI) IS NOW PROMINENT IN THE BEHAVIORAL health professions, being used in clinical, administrative, advocacy, policy, and educational contexts. Behavioral health practitioners are using AI to provide clinical services and interventions, conduct risk assessments, forecast clinical outcomes, and address potential and actual systemic bias in the delivery of services and employee hiring. Increasing numbers of behavioral health practitioners are using AI to document clinical services, provide training and supervision, and educate students.

These are impressive developments. That said, AI comes with noteworthy ethical challenges and legal risks. Key challenges include issues of informed consent and client autonomy; privacy and confidentiality; transparency; client misdiagnosis; client abandonment; client surveillance; plagiarism, dishonesty, fraud, and misrepresentation; and algorithmic bias and unfairness (Plante, 2023; Reamer, 2023a; Rubeis, 2022; Tambe & Rice, 2018; Terra et al., 2023).

This book has several goals. First, I provide a brief history of AI and explore its diverse uses in behavioral healthcare.* Second, I provide an overview of key ethical issues and challenges associated with behavioral health practitioners' use of AI. Third, I discuss ethics-informed "best practices" associated with behavioral health practitioners' use of AI, including guidelines

* My discussion of AI tools includes references to specific platforms and products. My references to these AI platforms and products are for illustrative purposes; they are not endorsements.

and protocols that practitioners and program administrators can use to ensure the ethical use of AI. I then discuss a wide range of risk management issues associated with practitioners' use of AI, including practical ways to protect clients and prevent malpractice litigation and licensing board complaints.* Throughout the discussion I include case examples to illustrate key concepts.**

HISTORY AND NATURE OF ARTIFICIAL INTELLIGENCE

The term *artificial intelligence* was introduced in 1955 by Stanford University professor John McCarthy (Petrosyan, 2024; Reamer, 2023a). Today, AI draws on computer science and datasets to simulate human intelligence and enable problem solving in a wide variety of settings, including behavioral health. AI includes what is known as *machine learning* (ML), which uses historical data to predict and shape new output. The term *generative AI* refers to the creation of images, videos, audio, text, and 3D models using learning patterns from existing data to generate new content and outputs. According to Copeland (n.d.), AI is the ability of digital computers or a computer-controlled robot to perform tasks commonly associated with intelligent beings.

AI can include what are known as expert systems, natural language processing, speech recognition, and machine vision (i.e., the ability of machines to see, analyze, and act). AI uses algorithms to generate responses to queries and provide guidance and suggestions. In healthcare professions, such as medicine and nursing, AI has been used to diagnose disease, facilitate patient treatment, automate redundant tasks, document clinical encounters, provide customer service, reduce dosage errors, provide robot-assisted services, analyze patient scans, and detect fraud (Rong et al., 2020).

More specifically related to behavioral health, what is known as *affective computing* and *emotion AI* apply this technology to practitioners' efforts to assist struggling individuals and those who support them (Diez, 2023; Luxton, 2016; Pascoe, 2023; Royer, 2021). Key AI options include chatbots,

---

* My discussion of risk management issues includes references to laws (for example, statutes, regulations, case law) and legal concepts related to the use of AI. I am not an attorney and cannot offer legal advice. My advice is limited to ethical and risk management issues. If you feel the need for legal consultation on these and related issues, please consult an attorney licensed in your jurisdiction who has expertise pertaining to the topics addressed in this book.

** In this book, I use pseudonyms in case examples to protect the identities of the clients.

social robots, machine translation, search engines, predictive analytic tools, speech-to-text tools, text recognition, speech generation, image recognition and generation, and research tools to assist people who struggle with mental health, substance use disorders, and other behavioral health challenges.

Chatbots

A *chatbot* is a computer program that simulates human conversation to solve users' queries. When an individual who is struggling with a behavioral health issue reaches out, the chatbot is there to welcome them and address their problems. Some chatbots connect users with a human agent. These conversational agents can hold discussions with users in the form of text, voice, or a combination of both. For example, a chatbot might provide a user who is experiencing depression or anxiety with assessment questions, self-help suggestions, resources, and referrals. Chatbots use *natural language processing*, which entails speech recognition and text analysis to simulate human conversations via computer programs and create and understand clinical documentation.

If security measures are lax, unauthorized access to chatbot data can lead to a data breach. Chatbot developers must explore encryption options to prevent unauthorized access to sensitive information about, among other things, users' personal lives, mental health symptoms, substance use, health challenges, financial and legal problems, and trauma history. The communication channel between the user and the chatbot in addition to the chatbot data themselves can also be a target for attacks. If the data transmission is inadequately encrypted, data could be intercepted by third parties, leading to the potential exposure of sensitive information.

Two unique risks with chatbots are referred to as (1) *model inversion attacks* in which an attacker reconstructs sensitive data shared during a chatbot exchange and (2) *adversarial attacks* in which slight changes to input data can cause the model to make incorrect decisions or reveal sensitive information. Another risk is an *injection attack* in which someone introduces malicious data that the chatbot mistakenly processes, thus allowing unauthorized access to sensitive data by third parties.

Chatbot developers must be cognizant of ethical issues related to unauthorized access, implementation of regular security audits, compliance with federal and state privacy statutes and regulations, and the possibility that users will insert malicious code or scripts.

Case 1.1: Terrance L. and the Chatbot

A 42-year-old man, Terrance L. recently separated from his wife after 20 years of marriage. He was struggling with intense feelings of loneliness and sadness. Suspecting he might be depressed, Terrance logged on to a behavioral health website featuring a chatbot that incorporates key features of cognitive–behavioral therapy (CBT). He engaged the chatbot, which led him through a series of questions about his unique circumstances, feelings, and symptoms. The chatbot provided Terrance with empathic responses and suggested some breathing exercises, self-help ideas, and online resources. The chatbot also encouraged Terrance to consult with a local psychiatrist to explore possible medication.

In his exchanges with the chatbot, Terrance disclosed many personal and intimate details about his life. The behavioral health organization that sponsors the chatbot has an ethical duty to alert Terrance to risks associated with these disclosures, obtain Terrance's informed consent to participate in the chatbot exchanges, and take constructive steps to ensure protection of Terrance's privacy.

Social Robots

A *social robot* is a robot capable of interacting with humans and other robots. Social robots can provide emotional support, companionship, and personal assistance services to older adults, people with disabilities, children with special needs, and other vulnerable populations. Social robots are developed using AI and are often equipped with sensors, cameras, microphones, and other technology so they can respond to touch, sounds, and visual cues much like humans would. Using AI, a robot can decipher facial expressions, engage in conversations, respond with a smile, read text and email messages, place video calls, tell stories and jokes, and track humans with their eyes to prove it is paying attention.

Social robots use AI to gather information from users, such as nursing home residents and vulnerable people who live independently. Thus, it is important for developers to address ways to protect the privacy of this information and prevent discrimination based on race, ethnicity, national origin, religion, sexual orientation, gender expression, disability, or other personal factors. Behavioral health professionals who use social robots must explore the extent to which clients understand that these devices are mimicking human emotion and expression and cannot truly empathize with clients. For clients who struggle with cognitive impairment or other challenges, practitioners must be specifically concerned about the extent to which their own use of social robots is deceptive and misleading.

Case 1.2: Emma S. and Social Robots

Emma S. is the director of social services at a nursing home where many of the residents struggle with social isolation and some form of cognitive impairment. Emma recently attended a workshop session at a professional conference that provided an overview of the ways in which some nursing homes are using "social robots" and AI to serve residents. The life-size social robot is dressed in human-style clothing and, using AI software, interacts with nursing home residents.

Behavioral health organizations that use social robots featuring AI software are obligated to consider relevant ethical issues and implications. These include the possibility that clients, especially those who are cognitively impaired, will be misled about the fact that they are not communicating with a human being. Further, behavioral health organizations that provide services to clients using social robots must comply with prominent ethical standards concerning informed consent. For clients who are not competent to provide consent, behavioral health organizations must ensure that a surrogate decision maker recognized by law has the authority to provide proxy consent on the client's behalf.

Machine Learning and Translation

ML is a branch of AI and computer science that focuses on the use of data and algorithms to enable AI to imitate the way that humans learn. Over time, ML uses these data to gradually improve its accuracy. According to the University of California–Berkeley School of Information (UC Berkeley, 2020), ML involves using statistical learning and optimization methods that let computers analyze datasets and identify patterns. ML techniques use what is known as *data mining* to identify historical trends and inform future models. Since ML algorithms update autonomously, in theory, the accuracy improves with each run as the algorithm teaches itself from the data it analyzes. This is called *iteration*.

There are several ML models: supervised learning, unsupervised learning, semisupervised learning, and reinforcement learning (UC Berkeley, 2020):

Supervised learning: The dataset being used has been prelabeled and classified by users to allow the algorithm to see how accurate its performance is.

Unsupervised learning: The raw dataset being used is unlabeled, and an algorithm identifies patterns and relationships within the data without help from users.

Semisupervised learning: The dataset contains structured and unstructured data to help the algorithm make independent conclusions. The combination of the two data types in one training dataset allows ML algorithms to learn to label unlabeled data.

Reinforcement learning: The dataset uses "rewards" and "punishment," which provide feedback to the algorithm to learn from its own experiences by trial and error.

The typical supervised ML algorithm consists of three components (UC Berkeley, 2020):

1. **A decision process:** A recipe of calculations or other steps that takes in the data and "guesses" what kind of pattern the user's algorithm is looking to find.

2. **An error function:** A method of measuring how good the software's guess was by comparing it with known examples.

3. **An updating or optimization process:** A method in which the algorithm looks at the "miss" (inaccurate guess) and then updates how the decision process comes to the final decision to minimize "misses" in the future.

In addition, the concept of *deep learning* involves automatically learning from datasets without introducing human rules or knowledge. This requires massive amounts of raw data for processing; the more data that are received, the more the predictive model improves (UC Berkeley, 2020). Deep learning relies on what are known as *deep neural networks* that are trained on large datasets to identify and classify phenomena, recognize patterns and relationships, evaluate possible responses to queries, and make predictions and decisions.

In behavioral health, ML software is designed to enhance accuracy in diagnosing mental health conditions and predicting client outcomes. For example, users who seek information to help them cope with mood disorders or anxiety can submit queries to chatbots that engage in dialogue and generate diagnostic questions, conduct assessments, and suggest treatment options and resources.

Behavioral health professionals who rely on ML and translation must address potential ethical issues related to the privacy and surveillance of users' data, possible bias and discrimination resulting from AI's use of historical data, and threats to users' autonomy if results from ML make decisions for them.

Case 1.3: Melinda G. and ML

Melinda G. was in recovery after many years of struggling with her addiction to heroin. She was on probation following her arrest for shoplifting and possession of heroin with intent to sell. As a condition of probation, Melinda was required to participate in an outpatient substance use disorders treatment program.

Melinda missed three of her previous five counseling appointments; twice, she overslept, and once, her car would not start. The director of the treatment program notified Melinda that she was being terminated from the program due to her attendance problems. Melinda knew that this termination would violate her probation conditions, which might lead to her arrest and incarceration. She felt desperate for help and looked online for crisis intervention services. Melinda connected with an online crisis intervention service that uses AI. The AI software was developed using a "reinforcement learning" model, which posed a series of questions to Melinda and offered responses to help her manage her crisis. The algorithm used Melinda's responses as feedback and made adjustments accordingly throughout their online exchange.

Behavioral health organizations that use AI-based reinforcement learning to serve clients must consider key ethical issues, including the possibility that some clients may not understand fully that this software may surveil and monitor clients' behaviors, emotions, and activities. Further, AI-generated responses to clients may reflect algorithmic bias that discriminates based on demographic factors, such as race, ethnicity, gender, income, sexual orientation, and gender expression. This would violate behavioral health practitioners' ethical duty to not discriminate against clients.

Search Engines

Powerful *search engines* use natural language processing and ML to enhance the quality of results provided in response to users' queries. Moving beyond popular search engines, such as Bing and Google, sophisticated search engines (e.g., Andi, Brave, Perplexity, Phind, and You) use natural language processing and ML to generate text and image results. For example, users can post questions about behavioral health challenges they are experiencing and receive detailed information about diagnostic criteria, treatment options, and resources.

Behavioral health practitioners who use sophisticated search engines must address ethical issues related to possible reliance on inaccurate or false information, manipulation of search engine results and rankings, privacy risks associated with search engines' collection of users' data, use of search engine queries for surveillance purposes, and violation of copyright law.

Case 1.4: Tess R. and Search Engines

Tess R. is a transgender woman who recently transitioned. She was distressed that her parents were not supportive of her decision and found herself engaging in suicidal thoughts. She logged on to a search engine and posed the question, "What kind of help is there for people who are having suicidal thoughts?" Within seconds, the search engine provided Tess with guidance under several major headings: direct support and professional help, connecting with support services, action steps for communicating with someone who may be suicidal, psychotherapies (i.e., CBT and dialectical behavior therapy [DBT]), warning signs of suicide, resources and brochures, and links to crisis services.

Search engines' use of sophisticated natural language processing can clash with prominent ethical standards in the behavioral health professions (Reamer, 2023c). In theory, search engine results can mislead clients, provide them with inaccurate information, collect users' personal information without their full knowledge and consent, and be used against users during legal proceedings. Sponsors of search engines that rely on AI must comply with key ethical standards related to informed consent to ensure that users understand potential benefits and risks.

Predictive Analytic Tools

Predictive analytic tools use AI to extract insights from large volumes of data and forecast outcomes. Google Cloud BigQuery analyzes large datasets to find patterns that can help predict future behavior. Microsoft Azure Machine Learning helps organizations build, implement, and manage predictive models. Qlik Sense analyzes data to generate visualizations and insights to enhance decision making. SAP Predictive Analysis generates predictive models that can be used by organizations to make data-driven decisions. Sisense helps users explore data, create visualizations, and identify trends. TIBCO provides users with predictive analytics that can be used for decision making and to improve outcomes. MATLAB uses ML to analyze data and create simulations. Certilytics analyzes clinical episodes to help organizations identify opportunities for cost efficiencies, quality improvement, and enhanced client outcomes.

Behavioral health practitioners who rely on predictive analytic tools must explore ethical issues related to the possibility of inaccurate or misleading results, invasion of users' privacy, and systemic bias (based on these tools' use of historical data that may be linked to ethnic, racial, cultural, economic, political, sexual orientation, gender expression, and other forms of bias). One prominent example is the controversial use of AI predictive analytic tools in public child welfare agencies' decisions about foster care placements. According to Trail (2024):

> In the last decade, child welfare agencies have increasingly used big data to develop and implement predictive models to help them make decisions about the lives of children in foster care. With the goal of improving and making more consistent decisions, the models are attractive because the promise of better decisions should also lead to better outcomes for children. However, these models are far from perfect, and they have attracted criticism for their use of biased data, disregard of individual rights, and arbitrary weights. (para. 2)

The earliest versions of these predictive models were implemented in California and Illinois to predict potential child abuse, but the models produced so many false positive results that both states terminated the programs (Trail, 2024).

The AI-based child welfare risk model that is best known is the Allegheny [Pennsylvania] Family Screening Tool (AFST; Allegheny County Department of Human Services, 2016). Developers created a model using court records, records from child protective services, police, schools, and hospitals, and other public records to build a predictive model that creates a risk score for each child. When potential abuse is reported to the public child welfare hotline, screeners are given a predictive model score between 1 and 20 that represents the model's risk assessment for that child.

Proponents of the AFST claim that it reduces racial bias and accurately predicts cases of serious child injury. Critics say the model relies on biased public data, promotes racial overidentification of high-risk cases, relies heavily on historical family data that may not accurately reflect current circumstances, and has unintended negative effects on people with disabilities (Ballantyne, 2023; Dilorenzo, 2023; Seniutis et al., 2024; Trail, 2024).

Predictive analytic AI is also being used in criminal justice settings (Rogers, 2024; Russo et al., 2019) to identify high-risk individuals and to shape supervision and monitoring intensity levels. For example, individuals who are on parole can be equipped with smartphone monitors that gather the user's location data to ensure compliance with parole conditions (for example, a parolee who was convicted of a sex offense involving a child victim may be prohibited from certain geographic locations, such as schools and youth centers). Health-related AI can use a connected smartwatch to gather vital indicators like heart rate and temperature to detect when and how the user experiences acute stress. The AI software also provides users with reminders to report their stress levels and is designed to assess users' "healthy thinking patterns," employment activities, and coping strategies. The software's chatbot feature enables users to provide information on their status without direct interaction with their parole officer. The AI software uses what is known as *gamification* to incentivize parolees' positive behaviors: Gamification uses people's natural tendencies for competition, achievement, collaboration, and charity. Tools employed in game design, such as rewarding users for achievements, "leveling up," and earning badges or loyalty points, are used to motivate people to achieve their goals or boost performance (Rasure, 2021).

In substance use disorders treatment, AI is being used to match clients to their optimal therapeutic drug or combination of drugs, predict drug–target or drug–drug interactions, and optimize treatment protocols (Romm & Tsigelny, 2020). AI has also been used to analyze Facebook posts from people in outpatient addiction treatment and predict whether they will complete their program. In one study with mostly male participants, those who used language that referred to women in positive tones, which could indicate emotional support, left treatment less frequently than those who did not refer to women in positive tones. Researchers found that they could have predicted 79 percent of patients who did not finish the program (Lu, 2023).

One AI tool sends substance use disorders treatment clients a text, email, or push notification two days after being discharged from a program. Clients receive a link that prompts them to answer a few questions and then respond to an open-ended question by recording a video of themselves. The AI technology screens the videos submitted by clients and monitors speech patterns, language, movement, and so on. The tool, which can summarize the tendencies of a specific population as well as individuals, is designed to recognize the signs of a relapse or struggle. Human providers can use the information gathered via AI and reach out asynchronously with support and resources to prevent relapses before they occur (Gonzales, 2023).

An ambitious use of AI to address homelessness was undertaken by the University of Southern California Center for AI in Society (USC Center for AI in Society; Carroll, 2023; Rice et al., 2023). The AI triage tool developed by this group includes an assessment to gauge the extent and nature of clients' needs and vulnerability. The researchers identified 19 questions that would most accurately predict future adverse events for a client and the client's likelihood of exiting homelessness. This group worked with an advisory board to generate items that are sensitive to trauma and racism experienced by many people who struggle with homelessness. These researchers also created guidelines designed to reduce client stress during the intake process and increase the likelihood that respondents will be forthcoming about the challenges they experience.

Case 1.5: Leah D. and Predictive AI Tools

Leah D. is the clinical director of an outpatient psychiatric clinic that provides services to people experiencing challenges related to mood, anxiety, relationship conflict, and substance use. Leah was eager to conduct an in-depth analysis of clinical outcomes experienced by clients who terminated services within the past three years. She consolidated the program's discharge summaries for these former clients and used predictive analytic software to summarize trends and forecast outcomes, including key correlates of positive results, for people experiencing common behavioral health challenges reflected in the clinic's client population.

Leah and her colleagues must consider ethical issues related to the possibility of inaccurate or misleading results, invasion of users' privacy, and systemic bias that can result from predictive analytic tools that use AI. Leah might appoint a clinic-based task force whose mission would be to identify these ethical issues and develop policies and protocols to mitigate these risks.

Speech-to-Text Tools

With *speech-to-text* tools, AI is used to convert speech into text. For example, Alrite, Microsoft Azure Speech to Text, Otter, and SpeechText use deep learning technology to transcribe audio. Some of these tools also transcribe video.

Behavioral health practitioners who rely on speech-to-text tools must explore ethical issues associated with possible error (poor translation from speech to text); bias and discrimination correlated with users' race, ethnicity, culture, accents, and disabilities; and deception as a result of voice cloning (misleading impersonation).

Case 1.6: Chris D. and Speech-to-Text Tools

Chris D. is a clinical social worker in private (independent) practice. They rely on speech-to-text AI software to generate their clinical notes following counseling sessions. Using deep learning, "domain-optimized" ML models, and speech recognition technology, the software allows clinicians to convert recorded clinical sessions to text, including automated punctuation features. The software allows clinicians to convert recorded clinical sessions to text—including automated punctuation features—which is stored on a secure cloud infrastructure. Editing tools allow clinicians to search, modify, and verify audio transcriptions.

Like many clinicians, Chris uses AI software to generate their clinical notes, which can save them considerable time. However, these tools come with several ethical risks. Ultimately, Chris is responsible for ensuring that the AI-generated clinical notes are thorough and accurate and incorporate all of their clinically relevant observations. Failure to proofread and edit the notes carefully could expose Chris to considerable risk.

Text Recognition

A *text recognition* AI tool recognizes patterns in text and enhances the quality of users' writing. For example, QuillBot can analyze blog posts, research papers, and other written documents to identify patterns and detect repetitive words, awkward phrasing, and unnatural flow. Google Cloud Vision API can extract text from images and documents and digitize printed materials. Tesseract OCR and Amazon Textract can recognize text from images and scanned documents. ABBYY FineReader can convert scanned documents, images, and PDFs into editable formats. Behavioral health practitioners who use text recognition software must explore ethical issues related to perpetuation of stereotypes because of the tool's use of historical data, protection of users' privacy, plagiarism and copyright violations, and reliance on inaccurate information.

Case 1.7: Deborah S. and Text Recognition

Deborah S. is the principal investigator in a large study of the effectiveness of clinical interventions for adults diagnosed with co-occurring disorders (for example, substance use disorders along with other behavioral health challenges). As part of the study, a large sample of behavioral health clinicians documented summaries of their clinical methods and protocols along with client outcomes. Deborah plans to use AI text recognition software to identify prominent patterns in this large volume of summaries and edit the summaries to enhance clarity.

Deborah and her colleagues will need to be keenly aware that this AI tool has the potential to promote stereotypes based on its use of historical and possibly biased data. They will need to be vigilant in their efforts to keep an eye out for these ethical problems as they use text recognition software.

Speech Generation

A wide range of tools use AI to convert text to speech; examples include Altered, Listnr, LOVO AI, Murf AI, Synthesia, VoiceOverMaker, and Voiser. Behavioral health practitioners who rely on text to speech software should explore ethical issues related to voice cloning and impersonation; invasion of users' privacy; bias associated with users' race, ethnicity, culture, accents, and disabilities; fraud and data manipulation; and plagiarism and copyright violations.

Case 1.8: Latetia T. and Speech Generation

Latetia T. is the training director and quality control manager for a psychiatric hospital in a large metropolitan community. Her responsibilities include designing and delivering staff development trainings on topics such as cultural diversity, employee burnout and self-care, and professional ethics. To enhance efficiency, Latetia uses AI to convert the text of the scripts for her training sessions to speech so that staffers can hear the trainings when convenient. The AI software she uses generates realistic intonations and creates an avatar from her uploaded photos.

Latetia must recognize that use of speech generation software that incorporates AI runs the risk of generating speech that does not accurately reflect the text on which it is based. This requires diligent review of the AI-generated audio.

Image Recognition and Generation

With *image recognition and generation*, AI tools can be used to recognize images and generate avatars to resemble human beings. Examples of image recognition tools include Azure Machine Learning, BoofCV, OpenCV, Python, SimpleCV, TensorFlow, and YOLOv7. Examples of image generation tools include Pixlr and Synthesia. Computer vision analyzes images and nonverbal cues generated by clients, such as facial expression, gestures, and eye gaze, to analyze clients' communications and clinicians' responses. Behavioral health practitioners who use image recognition and generation software should explore ethical issues associated with use of personal information without consent; surveillance (for example, facial recognition technology); bias associated with users' race, ethnicity, culture, accents, and disabilities; and fraud and data manipulation.

Case 1.9: Jackson D. and Image Recognition and Generation

Jackson D. is clinical director of a substance use disorders treatment program. One of his duties is to provide clinical supervision to staffers who are seeking licensure. As part of the supervision, Jackson has supervisees video-record a sample of their clinical sessions (with client consent). Jackson then uses AI image recognition software to analyze clients' nonverbal cues and clinicians' responses. Jackson also uses image generation software to create an option for his program's clients to engage in synchronous (real-time) counseling sessions with clinicians. For this option, both clinicians and clients create avatars that are animated during clinical encounters.

The use of image recognition and generation software can lead to diverse ethics challenges. Jackson and his colleagues will need to be alert to the possibility that this form of AI can lead to the use of personal information without truly informed consent and lead to algorithmic bias. Ideally, they will develop a protocol to monitor and minimize these risks.

Research Tools

Behavioral health practitioners, educators, and scholars have access to powerful *research tools* that use AI to locate professional literature and assess the quality of studies. For example, Scite uses AI to evaluate the reliability of scientific studies. Trinka uses AI to help draft research papers. Elicit uses AI to mine information from research papers and summarize key findings. Scholarcy uses AI to generate summaries of research papers. IBM Watson uses AI to provide data analysis assistance and language translation.

Behavioral health practitioners who rely on AI to conduct research should explore ethical issues associated with data privacy and breaches; misrepresentation of research results; bias associated with research participants' race, ethnicity, culture, sexual orientation, gender expression, and disabilities (biased samples); fraud and data manipulation; unwarranted generalization of results across populations and cultures; privileging certain kinds of research over others (for example, giving preference to quantitative studies over qualitative studies); and ensuring review of representative studies and literature (for example, including bodies of knowledge from underrepresented regions, populations, languages, and fields of study).

Case 1.10: Lindsey B. and AI Research Tools

Lindsey B. is a PhD student in a university's clinical social work program and is especially interested in studying the effectiveness of interventions for people who have been diagnosed with schizophrenia and experience homelessness. Lindsey logged on to an AI resource that summarizes major research papers on this topic and then uploaded a large number of research papers. The AI software provided succinct summaries and assessed the reliability of empirical studies.

College students, faculty, and agency-based researchers must recognize ethical risks associated with AI-dependent research tools. Lindsey should recognize that AI can misrepresent research results and be misleading about research design flaws and limitations, such as biased samples and weak research methodology. Users of these research tools must continually assess the quality, validity, and reliability of the AI-generated results.

USES OF ARTIFICIAL INTELLIGENCE IN BEHAVIORAL HEALTHCARE

To develop ethics and risk management guidelines specifically for practitioners, it is important to appreciate the diverse ways in which AI is being used in the behavioral health professions. This context will inform the development of ethics-based protocols. In general, in behavioral health, AI is being used in five ways: to (1) provide clinical services; (2) document clinical services and encounters; (3) perform administrative tasks and functions; (4) conduct research and program evaluations; and (5) educate, train, and supervise students and practitioners.

Clinical Services

In clinical behavioral healthcare—the context in which AI has been especially prominent—this technology is serving various purposes. Most commonly, AI is being used to conduct risk assessments, provide crisis intervention services, design and implement prevention services and programs, identify and address systemic biases in the delivery of behavioral health services, screen job applicants, provide behavioral health training and education, and predict practitioner burnout and service outcomes (Asakura et al., 2020; Gillingham, 2019; Grządzielewska, 2021; Jacobi & Christensen, 2023; Keddell, 2019; Lanier et al., 2020; Liedgren et al., 2016; Molala & Mbaya, 2023; Reamer, 2023a; Rice et al., 2018; Schneider & Seelmeyer, 2019; Søbjerg, 2022; Tambe & Rice, 2018). For example, The Trevor Project has partnered with Google.org to launch the Crisis Contact Simulator, a counselor training tool powered by AI (Trevor News, 2024). The model simulates digital conversations with LGBTQ+ youths in crisis and enables counselors to experience realistic practice scenarios before using the technology to assist at-risk youths.

Woebot is another prominent AI tool. It uses natural language processing and learned responses to simulate therapeutic conversation, draw on the content of past sessions, and provide advice related to mood disorders and other behavioral health challenges.

Wysa is an AI service that responds to the emotions individuals express by using evidence-based CBT techniques, DBT, meditation, breathing, yoga, and motivational interviewing. The Heyy app gives users access to self-assessments and research-backed resources on emotional well-being along with links to behavioral health professionals who may be able to provide assistance. The meditation app Headspace features an AI tool called "Ebb" that helps the user process thoughts, feelings, and emotions. Pyx Health offers an app that is designed to engage and communicate with people who feel lonely. ChatGPT and Copilot offer people nearly instant suggestions of ways to address their emotional discomfort and distress, including ways to increase relaxation, enhance sleep, reduce caffeine and alcohol consumption, avoid negative thoughts, reduce risky behaviors, and receive support from friends and family.

Some of the most ambitious AI tools have been developed to provide behavioral health supports to members of the military and to military veterans. For example, the PTSD Coach app is a mobile application designed to help veterans and service members manage symptoms of PTSD. The app provides tools and resources to assist users in coping with PTSD symptoms commonly associated with military service, including anxiety, depression, and sleep challenges. This app offers users an interactive self-assessment tool that helps them track their symptoms over time. It also provides users with strategies to manage symptoms when they occur. The app includes audio-guided relaxation exercises and a virtual coach that can help users develop coping skills and set personal goals. In addition, it provides access to resources, such as crisis hotlines, support groups, and helpful websites.

The AIMS [Anger and Irritability Management Skills] app is a mobile application designed to help veterans and military service members manage feelings of anger and irritability. The app provides a variety of tools and resources to help users identify what leads them to experience anger and develop strategies for managing their complex emotions. AIMS also offers a self-assessment tool to track anger symptoms over time along with interactive exercises to teach relaxation techniques and problem-solving skills. Users can create a personalized anger management plan and set goals and strategies to manage their anger in a variety of challenging situations. The app provides a journaling feature to track progress and identify areas for improvement.

Users can learn skills to improve communication, strengthen relationships, and reduce stress levels.

Mindfulness Coach is an app that provides guided mindfulness exercises that can be tailored by users to their individual needs and preferences. It offers a range of exercises, including body scans, breathing exercises, and guided meditations, which can help users reduce stress, manage anxiety, and improve overall well-being. Users can set reminders to practice mindfulness throughout the day, track progress over time, and customize exercises. The app can customize mindfulness exercises to specific challenges that users experience, such as managing symptoms of PTSD, depression, or anxiety. The app also provides resources and guidance to help users develop a mindfulness practice that can be incorporated into their daily routine.

Annie, the mobile app from the U.S. Department of Veterans Affairs is a text messaging tool designed to facilitate self-care for veterans. Clients using Annie receive automated prompts to track and monitor their own health. The app also provides users with motivational and educational messages. The Annie App for Clinicians allows behavioral health practitioners to use and create care protocols that allow clients to submit their health readings back to Annie. Clinicians can view these texts and data within the Annie App for Clinicians as needed.

Case 1.11: Aaliyah S. and AI in Clinical Services

Aaliyah S. is the clinical director at a university counseling center. Due to budget constraints, Aaliyah has had to lay off two of the center's seven full-time clinicians. She is very concerned about the increasing number of students who have sought counseling services and have had to be placed on a waiting list. In an effort to serve these students, Aaliyah contacted an AI company that markets a chatbot that serves as an automated therapist.

One can certainly understand why Aaliyah is tempted to expand the services she offers students using an automated therapist. For both ethical and risk management purposes, Aaliyah must identify and address risks that can occur when an automated therapist does not adequately address students' emotional crises in a timely fashion, provides misleading or inaccurate advice, or does not provide students with appropriate recommendations and resources.

Documentation

Several AI *documentation* tools are available to generate clinicians' notes that summarize their client encounters. Typical protocols require clinicians to record in-person and remote counseling sessions (with clients' consent) with a built-in recorder and upload the recordings to the AI platform. The software can also generate notes from telephone sessions with clients. The AI platform "listens" to the recording and produces a clinical note using a format of the clinician's choosing (for example, DAP, SOAP, BIRP, PIRP). Some AI documentation software provides therapists with detailed statistics on recorded audio sessions, such as session duration, client–therapist speaking time, and silent periods. Examples include AWS HealthScribe, Eleos, Epic, and Mentalyc.

Case 1.12: Carissa D. and AI Documentation

Carissa D. is the owner of a group private practice. For years, she has listened to her clinicians complain about the amount of uncompensated time they need to spend documenting their encounters with clients. At a continuing education conference, Carissa learned that some of her colleagues had contracted with a company that enables clinicians to upload recorded clinical sessions to the company's platform, which uses proprietary AI technology to review the recording and generate the clinical notes.

It is understandable that Carissa wants to ease her clinicians' documentation burden by using an AI product that generates clinical notes. However, she must implement rigorous risk management protocols to minimize the possibility that AI-generated clinical notes are not entirely accurate and thorough. Carissa must also ensure that the software fully protects sensitive and confidential information shared by clients during clinical sessions.

Administrative Tasks and Functions

At the programmatic level, predictive analytics—the use of data for forecasting service successes and challenges—can help agency administrators understand how best to respond to clients' needs and allocate scarce resources. For example, DataKind has worked with food pantries to analyze historical data using AI and ML algorithms to predict a client's level of dependency on the pantry. By mining data, DataKind has been able to prioritize resources and prevent food insecurity before it escalates (Goldkind, 2021). As another example, the National Fair Housing Alliance has identified ways in which AI is being used to predict which properties a potential tenant or buyer may be interested in; screen potential tenants and buyers considering their credit history, employment status, and rental history; and analyze potential tenants' and buyers' financial stability and risk (Petrosyan, 2024). This use of AI has profound implications for behavioral health clients who experience housing challenges and insecurity that may cause intense emotional distress.

Case 1.13: Audrey K. and AI in Administrative Tasks

Audrey K., a social worker, is executive director of a program that serves people experiencing homelessness. Her large staff of outreach workers and caseworkers records every client encounter with a smartphone app that summarizes the client's health and mental health status, imminent and long-term needs, services provided, and resources offered. Audrey was in the process of writing a grant application she planned to submit to a national foundation. She wanted to include a summary of the services her organization provided during the preceding year to forecast future trends. She hired a consultant who is skilled at employing AI to mine data using historical information from the organization's database to predict future demands for its services.

To protect clients and her program, Audrey must develop policies and protocols that comply with ethical standards related to informed consent and protection of sensitive and confidential information shared by clients and recorded on staffers' smartphone apps. She would be wise to confer with the consultant about ways to prevent algorithmic bias when the AI software predicts future demands for agency services.

Research and Program Evaluation

Powerful AI tools are used by behavioral health researchers and program evaluators to design studies, collect data (for example, using automated interviews and questionnaires), and analyze data (for example, identifying patterns in qualitative data generated by respondents, ranking and prioritizing data). One such tool, CRISbot (Conversational Research Insight System), is a virtual moderator that uses AI to conduct text-based interviews and collect both qualitative and quantitative data on a web-based messaging platform. The software assesses respondents' "sentiments" and facilitates discussion.

The USC Center for AI in Society has been demonstrating innovative ways that AI can be used to address compelling behavioral health challenges (Carroll, 2023). The primary goal of the center is to develop, test, iterate, and demonstrate how AI can be used to study compelling social and behavioral health problems. This ambitious and creative initiative entails close collaboration among computer science, operations research, social work, and community organizations. Projects use AI to study ways to, among other social and behavioral health issues, prevent substance use among youths experiencing homelessness; prevent suicide among active-duty military personnel, youths experiencing homelessness, and college students; prevent HIV among youths experiencing homelessness; and match housing options with people experiencing homelessness.

Case 1.14: Carl F. and AI in Program Evaluation

Carl F., a mental health counselor, is director of quality assurance for a community mental health center. A federal agency that provides funds to the center requires annual collection of client satisfaction data. Carl and their staff have used a standardized client satisfaction survey tool that they administer to all active clients every six months and a separate survey that the center administers to all clients who have terminated services. Both instruments collect qualitative and quantitative data. To facilitate the data analysis, Carl contracted with a research firm that uses AI software to analyze the qualitative data describing clients' experiences to identify themes and patterns.

AI software offers powerful tools for analysis of qualitative data. Carl would be wise to monitor the accuracy of the AI-generated results to prevent any misrepresentation of respondents' comments. One possibility is for Carl to appoint a task force that would identify a representative sample of the AI-generated results and, for quality control purposes, compare them with clients' actual responses to questions about the services they received.

Education, Training, and Supervision

Behavioral health educators and trainers can use AI software to teach students, train staffers, and supervise students and employees. Typical protocols include recording students' and supervisees' client encounters (with client consent) and uploading the recording to the AI platform (Reamer, 2023a). For example, the AI platform Lyssn is designed to assess and improve fidelity to evidence-based clinical interventions. Lyssn reviews each interaction and applies a large number of clinically and externally validated measurements of fidelity. For instance, when clinicians use motivational interviewing, the AI software creates ratings of the therapeutic relationship, clinician empathy, active listening, advice-giving, collaboration, affirmations, and client change language. When clinicians provide CBT, the software creates specific subscales, such as agenda-setting, collaboration, interpersonal effectiveness, guided discovery, and homework. The software also generates summaries of time spent on key clinical topics, including discussions of mood, substance use, and interpersonal relationships.

In professional education programs, AI is being used to detect plagiarism. Typical software reviews students' uploaded papers and looks for unoriginal content by identifying areas of overlap between submitted assignments and existing works that are online. The software creates a digital fingerprint of the content of a paper using a *hash*, a type of mathematical algorithm (a hash function garbles data so that they cannot be read by other parties). This digital footprint is unique to each student's paper and is used to compare it with different sources. The AI software then compares this digital fingerprint to content submitted by other users as well as its own database of journals and websites, looking for matching or similar text. The software generates an *originality report* that highlights any areas of potential plagiarism along with a percentage of similarity. The report also includes a list of sources used. An instructor can look at the report to determine whether a reference was improperly cited or if plagiarism has occurred.

Case 1.15: Alexandra M. and AI in Supervision

Alexandra M. is director of internship training at a marriage and family therapy institute. Students enrolled in the institute's graduate degree program complete practicums at local behavioral health agencies. Alexandra recently read an article in a professional journal about AI software that some training programs are using to provide clinicians with feedback about their clinical skills. The software reviews recordings of counseling sessions and provides detailed comments on the extent to which clinicians used a wide range of core clinical skills.

Used properly, AI is a powerful tool for education, training, and supervision. The challenge for Alexandra is to ensure that whatever AI tool she uses to provide clinicians with feedback has been validated and produces reliable results to ensure compliance with ethical standards related to responsible supervision.

CONCLUSION

AI is transforming behavioral health and is now an option in a wide range of behavioral health settings that serve a broad range of clients. AI is being used to provide clinical services; document clinical services and encounters; perform administrative tasks and functions; conduct research and program evaluations; and educate, train, and supervise students and practitioners.

The rapid proliferation of AI in the behavioral health professions has produced novel and unprecedented ethical and risk management challenges. I now turn to a discussion of these complex issues.

2

Ethical Issues in the Use of Artificial Intelligence in Behavioral Health

Behavioral healthcare practitioners who use AI face a number of key ethical considerations related to informed consent and client autonomy; privacy and confidentiality; transparency; client misdiagnosis; client abandonment; client surveillance; plagiarism, dishonesty, fraud, and misrepresentation; and algorithmic bias and unfairness (Ashok et al., 2022; Bankins & Formosa, 2023; Char et al., 2020; Chen et al., 2021; Giarmoleo et al., 2023; Grote & Berens, 2020; Hagendorff, 2020; Johnson, 2019; Li et al., 2023; Martin, 2019; Morley et al., 2020; Murphy et al., 2021; Orr & Davis, 2020; Reamer, 2023a; Wangmo et al., 2019). In this chapter, I explore each of these ethical considerations, present cases that arise in behavioral health, and explore the ethical implications for each.

INFORMED CONSENT AND CLIENT AUTONOMY

When using AI, practitioners should inform clients of relevant benefits and risks and respect clients' judgment about whether to accept or decline the use of AI. This expectation is reflected in prominent codes of ethics in the behavioral health professions. For example, the American Psychological Association (APA, 2017) *Ethical Principles of Psychologists and Code of Conduct* states:

> When psychologists . . . provide assessment, therapy, counseling, or consulting services in person or via electronic transmission or other forms of communication, they obtain the informed consent of the individual or individuals using language that is reasonably understandable

> to that person or persons except when conducting such activities without consent is mandated by law or governmental regulation or as otherwise provided in this Ethics Code. (Standard 3.10)

According to the National Association of Social Workers (NASW, 2021) *Code of Ethics*:

> Social workers who use technology to provide social work services should obtain informed consent from the individuals using these services during the initial screening or interview and prior to initiating services. Social workers should assess clients' capacity to provide informed consent and, when using technology to communicate, verify the identity and location of clients. (Standard 1.03[f])

One key ethical concern is that AI may reduce clients' autonomy by providing them with paternalistic advice in response to their queries. As Li et al. (2023) observed regarding the ethical implications of AI in healthcare settings:

> In the context of healthcare, the sub-issue of respecting human autonomy refers to the respect for patient autonomy. It could also be called respecting patient choice, recognizing the individual's ability for self-determination and the right to make choices based on their values and beliefs. The opacity of ML-based decisions can potentially threaten patients' autonomy by impairing the authority of physicians and the shared decision-making between doctors and patients. For instance, algorithms applied in healthcare enforce the paternalistic model by prescribing values on ranked treatment options, which ignore the patient's preferences and harm their autonomy. (p. 39)

Behavioral health practitioners have always understood their duty to explain the potential benefits and risks of services as part of the informed consent process (Barsky, 2019; Reamer, 2023d, 2024). The historical roots of informed consent can be found in ancient Greece, particularly in Plato's *Laws* (Plato, 1994–2000). The medieval French surgeon Henri de Mondeville also stressed the importance of obtaining a patient's consent and confidence (Berg et al., 2001; Reamer, 2023d). By the late 18th century, European and American physicians and scientists had begun to encourage professionals to share information and decision making with their patients; these original developments are directly applicable to behavioral health practitioners' use of AI (Berg et al., 2001; Reamer, 2023d). Clearly, informed consent norms have changed since then, and these changes are relevant to behavioral health practitioners' use of AI.

The 1957 case of *Salgo v. Stanford University* introduced the phrase "informed consent" (Berg et al., 2001). The plaintiff, who became paraplegic following a diagnostic procedure for a circulatory disturbance, alleged that his physician did not properly disclose ahead of time pertinent information regarding risks associated with the treatment.

Although states and local jurisdictions have different interpretations and applications of informed-consent standards, what constitutes valid consent by clients depends on prevailing legislation and case law (Berg et al., 2001; Reamer, 2023d). In general, *valid informed consent* requires that practitioners satisfy seven standards: (1) clients' decisions should not be coerced; (2) clients must be sufficiently competent to provide consent; (3) clients must consent to specific procedures or actions; (4) consent forms must contain key relevant information, for example, about potential benefits and risks; (5) clients must have the right to refuse or withdraw consent; (6) clients' decisions must be based on adequate information about the services or procedures to which the client is consenting; and (7) practitioners must provide clients with information about the potential benefits and risks of remote delivery of services. These prominent standards are directly applicable to behavioral health practitioners' use of AI.

Absence of Coercion and Undue Influence

Practitioners who want clients to use AI tools need to be aware that clients may be particularly susceptible to influence, especially if they are in the midst of a crisis; this may jeopardize the validity of their consent. Practitioners must be sure that their informed consent policies and protocols related to the use of AI are not coercive.

Capacity to Consent

Clients who consent to the use of AI tools must be sufficiently competent. Although it is not always easy for practitioners to assess clients' competence, ethicists have agreed on several key criteria (Reamer, 2023d). These include evidence of individuals' ability to make choices, comprehend factual issues, manipulate information rationally, appreciate their current circumstances, retain information, communicate their wishes, and reason and deliberate. These threshold criteria are relevant when behavioral health practitioners offer clients the opportunity to use AI tools.

Ethicists also are in agreement that no one should assume that any specific client group, such as children, older adults, or people with mental illness or intellectual disabilities, are incompetent, except for those who are unconscious (Reamer, 2023d). Rather, clients in some categories—perhaps children or individuals with severe intellectual disability—should be considered to have a greater *probability* of incapacity. This distinction is relevant when behavioral health practitioners seek clients' consent to use AI and develop protocols to assess whether users are sufficiently competent to use AI tools.

Consent to Specific Procedures

Behavioral health agencies often have clients sign general consent forms early in the treatment protocol. In a number of precedent-setting cases in the context of medical care, however, clients have challenged such blanket consent forms in court, claiming that they lacked specificity and failed to authorize interventions introduced subsequently (Reamer, 2023d). In *Winfrey v. Citizens & Southern National Bank* (1979), a Georgia woman challenged her physician's authority to perform a complete hysterectomy based on her consent to an exploratory operation. In *Darrah v. Kite* (1969) a father of a young child challenged a New York neurosurgeon's authority to conduct a ventriculogram on the child when the consent form referred only to "routine brain tests" and a workup. Professionals are thus advised not to assume that general consent forms are valid. Rather, consent forms should include specific details that refer to specific activities or interventions, for example, behavioral health practitioners' efforts to incorporate AI into their clinical protocols.

The language and terminology that appear on consent forms related to practitioners' use of AI must be understandable to clients, and clients should have ample opportunity to ask questions about the details that are included (Reamer, 2023d). Practitioners should avoid as much as possible the use of complex and technical jargon associated with the use of AI, such as "machine learning," "ecological momentary assessment," "data mining," and "algorithmic bias." Clients who do not have good command of English need particular care; practitioners should be aware that some clients who are able to speak English reasonably well (expressive language skill) may not be equally capable of understanding the language (receptive language skill). Having access to an interpreter in such instances is important when practitioners offer clients the opportunity to use AI tools. In addition, practitioners should be certain that clients who have auditory or visual impairments are provided with the assistance they need to provide informed consent pertaining to the use of AI.

Valid Forms of Consent

Consent may be written or verbal, although some state laws require written authorization (Reamer, 2023d). In addition, consent may be expressed or implied. *Expressed consent* entails explicit authorization by a client for a specific intervention or activity, such as the use of AI in the therapeutic relationship. *Implied consent* occurs when consent is inferred from the facts and circumstances surrounding a client's situation. An example is a client who answers questions that are part of an anonymous and voluntary client satisfaction survey generated by an AI chatbot. A reasonable assumption is that the client has consented to the activity.

Right to Refuse or Withdraw Consent

Practitioners should anticipate that some clients will refuse or withdraw consent regarding the use of AI. If a client refuses to provide consent, the practitioner should document the practitioner's efforts to obtain consent and the client's decision.

Adequate Information

Practitioners should include key information in their discussions with clients before obtaining consent. This includes information about the nature and purpose of the AI tool; the advantages and disadvantages of the AI tool; substantial, probable, or significant risks to the client, if any, associated with the use of AI; potential effects of the use of AI on the client's family, partner, job, social activities, and other aspects of the client's life; and alternatives to the use of AI.

This information about the use of AI tools must be presented to clients in understandable language (taking into consideration clients' learning disabilities, cognitive impairment, literacy, and English comprehension) without coercion or undue influence and in a manner that encourages clients to ask questions. Consent forms should also be dated and should include an expiration date. Consent forms without an expiration date may be considered invalid if the original signature was obtained long before the form was actually used.

Practitioners must also consider that obtaining informed consent about the use of AI entails more than having clients sign a form. Lawyers agree that consent is a process that requires the systematic disclosure of information to a client over time along with an opportunity to discuss with the client the forthcoming use of AI (Reamer, 2023d). Practitioners should ensure during discussions with their clients that clients understand the risks, benefits, and alternatives to any use of AI. As part of this process, practitioners must be especially sensitive to clients' cultural and ethnic differences related to the meaning of such concepts as self-determination, autonomy, and consent.

Consent for Remote Delivery of Services

The proliferation of remote behavioral health services, including the use of AI, has enhanced practitioners' ethical duty to ensure that clients fully understand the nature of these services and their potential benefits and risks (Reamer, 2021). Obtaining clients' truly informed consent can be especially difficult when practitioners never meet clients in person, which is common when people access AI tools to help them cope with challenges in their lives. Special challenges arise when minors access AI tools; laws around the world vary considerably regarding minors' right to obtain services from behavioral health professionals without parental knowledge or consent.

When behavioral health professionals provide services to clients remotely, the informed consent form should include statements that address

- the nature of the AI services that the practitioner will provide.
- possible benefits of AI tools.
- possible limitations of AI tools.
- differences between services provided by human beings and those provided by AI tools (including the fact that practitioners do not have access to potentially important nonverbal cues, such as a client's clinically relevant body language).
- the skills and equipment (such as computer specifications and smartphone applications) the client will need to use AI tools.
- the importance of privacy for both practitioner and client; describe steps clients can take to ensure privacy (such as limiting who has access to their sensitive AI communications).

- the possibility of technology failure and AI transmission interruption along with instructions in the event these occur.
- the possibility that stored AI data could be accessed by unauthorized people or companies, and the steps the practitioner will take to prevent this.
- an emergency response plan to address crises that may arise for clients who use AI tools; details may include names and telephone numbers of individuals the practitioner can contact, telephone numbers the client can call, and when the client should access care at the client's local hospital emergency department.
- steps practitioners will take if they believe that the client needs to access face-to-face services instead of AI-generated resources because of their clinical needs; include details about referral and termination-of-service protocols. (Reamer, 2023d)

Case 2.1: Yolanda M. and Informed Consent

Yolanda M., a clinical psychologist in private practice, attended a continuing education seminar on the emerging use of AI in behavioral health. After doing some independent research on available AI tools, Yolanda decided to provide her clients with the option to begin using a chatbot posted on her clinical practice's website. The chatbot invites users to summarize their behavioral health concerns and request AI-generated information about self-care options, virtual and in-person counseling opportunities, and other resources (for example, relevant websites, literature). During the continuing education seminar she attended, Yolanda learned that she would need to develop an informed consent protocol that would be shared online with each chatbot user.

To her credit, Yolanda enrolled in a continuing education seminar related to the use of AI. She is responsible for drawing on what she learned about state-of-the-art policies and procedures, including development and implementation of a sound informed consent protocol.

PRIVACY AND CONFIDENTIALITY

Behavioral health practitioners who use AI must be vigilant in their efforts to protect users' privacy and confidentiality. Clients' and other users' willingness to use AI tools to share intimate and deeply personal details about their lives reflects their belief that their practitioner will not share this information with others and will protect it to the greatest extent possible. Practitioners should be familiar with and apply strict ethical and legal standards to protect clients and prevent litigation and licensing board complaints.

Practitioners must understand the differences between the concepts of privacy and confidentiality as they pertain to the use of AI. *Privacy* refers to the right to noninterference in individuals' thoughts, knowledge, acts, associations, and property (Reamer, 2023d). Thus, individuals who use AI tools offered by behavioral health practitioners should have the opportunity to decide whether to share important details about their lives, for example, their emotional and behavioral challenges, trauma history, sexual orientation, gender expression, religious beliefs, and political ideology. Confidentiality rights arise when individuals entrust others with private information, including information shared by those who avail themselves of AI tools offered by behavioral health practitioners.

In addition, practitioners who invite users to share information using AI tools must be familiar with the potential implications of the concept of privileged communication. The right of *privileged communication*—which assumes that a professional cannot disclose confidential information without the client's consent—originated in British common law (Reamer, 2023d). Attorney–client privilege is the oldest among professional–client relationships. Now those served by other groups of professionals, such as physicians, psychiatrists, social workers, psychologists, mental health counselors, and clergy, are protected by this right.

Behavioral health practitioners who use AI need to understand the distinction between confidentiality and privilege. *Confidentiality* refers to the ethical standard that information shared by or pertaining to clients will not be shared with third parties without proper authorization. *Privilege* is a much narrower concept; it refers to the disclosure of confidential information during court or legal proceedings. In theory, attorneys can subpoena behavioral health practitioners' records that incorporate AI-generated information, known legally as electronically stored information (ESI).

Behavioral health practitioners sometimes receive requests for privileged information, which may include information generated by AI. Practitioners must understand that under some circumstances, judges may review AI-generated information in practitioners' possession and apply widely accepted legal criteria to determine whether to compel disclosure. Judges typically consider four conditions, originally proposed by the jurist John Henry Wigmore, when deciding whether information is privileged and ought to be protected (Reamer, 2023d):

1. The parties involved in the conversation assumed that it was confidential.
2. Confidentiality was an important element in this relationship.
3. The community recognizes the importance of this relationship.
4. The harm caused by disclosure of the confidential information would outweigh the benefits of disclosure during legal proceedings.

Regarding the first criterion, behavioral health practitioners who gather information using AI can reasonably assume that users expect that information that they share will be kept confidential. Further, a central tenet of behavioral health is that clients must be able to trust practitioners with the most personal details of their lives and that such trust is necessary if this relationship, including disclosure of information using AI, is to be meaningful and productive. In addition, the community at large generally accepts the assumption that relations between clients and behavioral health practitioners are important and valuable, thus satisfying Wigmore's third criterion. The fourth criterion, that the injury caused by disclosure of confidential information is greater than the benefit gained from disclosure, is ordinarily the most difficult to satisfy and triggers the greatest debate. This is a debate that certainly is relevant to the possible subpoena of AI-generated information during legal proceedings involving clients.

The most significant federal court decision with direct bearing on behavioral health practitioners is the landmark case of *Jaffe v. Redmond* (1996) in which the Supreme Court of the United States (U.S. Supreme Court) ruled that the clients of clinicians have the right to privileged communication in federal courts (Reamer, 2023d). This ruling has potentially profound implications for behavioral health practitioners who use AI. In this precedent-setting case, a police officer, Mary Lu Redmond, sought counseling from a clinical social worker after the officer killed Ricky Allen, a man involved in a fight. Redmond had responded to a fight at an apartment complex. She shot Allen, believing he was about to stab a man he was chasing. The administrator of Allen's estate filed suit in U.S. district court, alleging that Officer Redmond violated Allen's constitutional rights by using excessive force. During the discovery phase of the case (*discovery* is a pretrial procedure by which one party obtains information—facts and documents, for example—about the other), the plaintiff learned that Redmond participated in many counseling sessions with social worker Karen Beyer. The plaintiff sought access to Beyer's clinical record; Redmond objected, arguing that disclosure should be prevented because of a psychotherapist–patient privilege. The district court judge ruled that the Federal Rules of Civil Procedure (Yeazell et al., 2022) did not provide for a psychotherapist–client privilege and allowed the discovery of Beyer's clinical record, but neither Beyer nor Redmond complied with the request. The judge advised the jury that the refusal to turn over Beyer's notes could be considered a presumption that the content of the notes would have been unfavorable to the Respondent. Ultimately, this case reached the U.S. Supreme Court.

In its decision, the U.S. Supreme Court said that

> participants [in therapy] must be able to predict with some degree of certainty whether particular discussions will be protected. An uncertain privilege, or one which purports to be certain but results in widely varying applications by the courts, is little better than no privilege at all. (LII Legal Information Institute, n.d., letter para. 22)

This case is particularly important because it established—for the first time in U.S. legal history—that clinical social worker–client relationships are privileged in federal court proceedings; until the *Jaffe* decision only some state courts recognized social worker–client privilege. It is conceivable that this compelling court ruling would apply in instances in which attorneys subpoena AI-generated information that was a component of a client's psychotherapy or other request for behavioral health information or services. For example, this U.S. Supreme Court ruling may be relevant if a prosecutor seeks AI-generated data in the possession of a behavioral health practitioner that the prosecutor believes is evidence in a criminal court proceeding.

Behavioral health practitioners who are in possession of AI information generated by or about a client must understand that the *client* holds the privilege—not the behavioral health practitioner. Under well-established ethical guidelines, the practitioner has a duty to assert the client's privilege and protect relevant information from disclosure to the greatest extent possible. That said, over the years, both courts and statutes have identified a number of exceptions to the client's right of privileged communication. A number of these exceptions pertain to judicial proceedings, such as when a client introduces in court information that they have received counseling for emotional problems resulting from an automobile accident that has led to a suit for damages or when a practitioner's testimony about a client is required so the practitioner can defend against a suit filed by the client.

Disclosure of AI-generated privileged information may also be permissible when a client threatens to die by suicide; shares information in the presence of a third person; is a minor and is the subject of a custody dispute; is involved in criminal activity or has been abused or neglected; is impaired and may pose a threat to the public (for example, an actively alcoholic airline pilot or bus driver); has not paid their fees, and a collection agency is retained; threatens to injure a third party; or has informed the practitioner about plans to commit a serious crime. In theory, a client could disclose this information using AI, such as a chatbot or smartphone app. This information could also be embedded in clinical notes that were generated by AI software.

Cases in which clients admit or confess to commission of a crime when using AI can be particularly complex (Reamer, 2023d). On the one hand, practitioners may want to avoid undermining clients' trust by disclosing confidential information. After all, some clients seek assistance using AI for the express purpose of addressing their guilt feelings and sense of remorse about past misdeeds. Practitioners may not want to discourage these constructive efforts. At the same time, however, practitioners can understand the legitimate claim by the public that it has a right and need to know who perpetrated serious crimes, particularly those that have not led to an arrest. Practitioners must also recognize that codes of ethics in the behavioral health professions prohibit disclosure of confidential information when such disclosure would not prevent serious, imminent, and foreseeable harm in the future (for example, when a client tells a counselor that they committed a serious crime years earlier, and there is no evidence of a contemporaneous threat of harm). For instance, the NASW (2021) *Code of Ethics* states, "The general expectation that social workers will keep information confidential does not apply when disclosure is necessary to prevent serious, foreseeable, and imminent harm to a client or others" (Standard 1.07[c]).

Although statutes are relatively clear that behavioral health practitioners must disclose information shared by clients concerning abuse or neglect of children or older adults, they offer less guidance with respect to other crimes committed by clients. Behavioral health practitioners must consider the potential legal implications if clients who use AI disclose information about crimes they have committed. We can imagine that some individuals might use AI to reach out to behavioral health practitioners about the possibility of becoming a client and, in the context of this AI communication, disclose information about crimes they have committed, such as sexually abusing a minor. This information may also be included in AI-generated clinical notes.

Practitioners should also be careful to seek clients' permission (or, in the case of minors, the permission of a parent or guardian) or a court order before disclosing privileged information that is embedded in AI communications. Otherwise, the practitioner might be found liable for violating clients' right to privacy and confidentiality.

Behavioral health practitioners often are asked or ordered to disclose confidential information in the context of civil or criminal court proceedings (Reamer, 2023d). In theory, this information might have been obtained by practitioners during the course of AI communications or included in AI-generated clinical notes. Prominent examples include practitioners who are subpoenaed to testify in the following:

> **Malpractice cases in which a client has sued another practitioner (for example, a physician):** The defendant's lawyer may subpoena the client's practitioner to gain testimony about the client's mental status or about comments made during counseling sessions. This information might be embedded in AI-generated communications or AI-generated clinical notes. The defense lawyer may attempt to introduce evidence that the client's allegations merely reflect the client's emotional instability, psychiatric illness, vindictiveness, or irrational tendencies. The defense may also try to show that the client had mental health problems that predated the emotional injury that the client claims were caused by the defendant in the case. Defense lawyers may use a similar strategy in other tort or personal injury cases in which a practitioner's client claims to have been injured by the actions of another party (for example, as a result of an automobile or workplace accident).

Custody disputes in which one parent subpoenas a practitioner who has worked with one or both parents: The parent believes that the practitioner's testimony will support their claim (for example, testimony concerning comments made during AI-generated exchanges or stored in AI-generated clinical notes about one parent's allegedly abusive behavior).

Divorce proceedings in which one spouse subpoenas a practitioner: That spouse believes that the practitioner's testimony about confidential conversations embedded in AI-generated exchanges or stored in AI-generated clinical notes will support claims against the other spouse.

Criminal court cases involving subpoenaing a practitioner: A prosecutor or defense attorney subpoenas a practitioner to testify about the defendant's comments during counseling sessions embedded in AI-generated exchanges or stored in AI-generated clinical notes.

Case 2.2: Darryl W. and AI in Privacy and Confidentiality

Darryl W., a marriage and family therapist, provided counseling to a couple that was experiencing marital conflict. Darryl recently learned about an AI tool that generates clinical session notes. The AI tool "listens" to a recording of the clinical session uploaded by the therapist (with clients' consent) and generates the session notes. The recording that is made available to the company that markets the AI tool includes protected health information (PHI). Darryl was unsure about what steps the AI company takes to protect clients' privacy and confidentiality.

To protect clients and himself, Darryl should familiarize himself with ethics-based discussions of the potential benefits and risks associated with practitioners' use of AI tools that generate clinical notes. These discussions acknowledge the time-saving benefits of these AI tools and, as well, highlight potential risks related to, among other things, documentation errors and privacy breaches.

RESPONDING TO SUBPOENAS AND COURT ORDERS

Behavioral health practitioners' electronically stored data can be subpoenaed by several different parties. A *subpoena* is a written document issued by a court clerk or officer of the court (such as an attorney) that commands a person to appear in court at a specific place and time or produce specific documents, including ESI generated by AI exchanges and AI-generated clinical notes (Barsky, 2024; Reamer, 2023d). Although it may appear to be a court order and looks official, it typically is not signed by a judge and is not the same as a court order.

Behavioral health practitioners can be subpoenaed in two different ways. A *subpoena ad testificandum*, also known as an ordinary subpoena, literally means "to testify under penalty." It commands a person to appear at a particular location to give testimony. The most common use of a subpoena is to require a witness to attend a deposition or trial. In theory, a behavioral health practitioner could be subpoenaed to testify in person about the ways in which they use AI in their clinical practice and, specifically, with the client who is involved in a legal proceeding.

A *subpoena duces tecum*, also known as a subpoena for production of evidence, literally means "bring with you under penalty." It commands a person to appear at a particular location to bring a specified item, such as a client's clinical record or copies of electronically stored and digital communications (such as AI-generated exchanges and clinical notes) for use or examination in a legal proceeding. A subpoena duces tecum is used most often in civil lawsuits when one party to a lawsuit seeks production of documents from a third party during the discovery process. If a court is convinced that the document request is legitimate, it can order the production and disclosure of documents.

In the United States, law enforcement agencies can issue subpoenas for physical devices—such as smartphones, tablets, and computers—that may contain AI data or directly to companies that manage AI data. What are known as "administrative subpoenas," which do not require a judge's signature, can also be issued. Further, the 1986 federal Stored Communications Act (SCA) governs the disclosure of electronic communications stored by third-party service providers.

The 1986 SCA prohibits providers of an electronic communication service or a remote computing service from disclosing the contents of the information stored on their systems, except under certain circumstances. The SCA also prohibits unauthorized access to an electronic communication service. This law is relevant when a party requests information from a covered business whether in litigation against that entity or via a third-party subpoena. The SCA establishes procedures for requests by the government. While the SCA provides some exceptions, including one in which governmental entities may, pursuant to an ongoing criminal investigation, require disclosure of the contents of customers' electronic communications or subscriber information, it does not include an exception that allows disclosure of electronic communications in response to a civil discovery subpoena. This presents a problem for private litigants seeking information through the discovery process when the relevant information is stored only with the internet service provider.

Practitioners should never alter records after receiving a subpoena or records request. This includes ESI, such as AI. Record alteration can constitute what attorneys call spoliation (Reamer, 2023d). *Spoliation* is any act that renders potential evidence invalid either intentionally or through negligence. In the case of a document, for example, destroying, altering, or hiding it would be considered spoliation if the requested document is relevant to current litigation.

Spoliation of records, including ESI, can lead to serious consequences. Courts may review the altered document with an "adverse" inference against the spoliator and in favor of the opposing party. Further, spoliation can lead to dismissal of the wrongdoer's claim, entering of a judgment against the wrongdoer, exclusion of expert testimony, and imposition of a fine.

Behavioral health practitioners who are subpoenaed in conjunction with their use of AI may face a special dilemma concerning the disclosure of privileged information. If the practitioner works in a state that grants the right of privileged communication to behavioral health practitioners' clients, challenging the subpoena may be easier because the legislature has acknowledged the importance of the privilege (Reamer, 2023d). Also, contrary to the understanding of many practitioners, a legitimate response to a subpoena is to argue that the requested information should not be disclosed or can be obtained from some other source. A subpoena itself does not require a practitioner to disclose information. Instead, a subpoena is essentially a request for information, and it may be without merit (Reamer, 2023d). Practitioners who receive a subpoena demanding production of AI-generated information should immediately notify their client and ask the client whether they want to sign a release-of-information form or contest the subpoena in court. Challenging a subpoena of AI-generated information is appropriate, particularly if practitioners believe that the information is privileged, is not essential to the legal matter, or if they can argue that the information can be obtained from other sources.

Lawyers typically offer several guidelines concerning the proper service of and response to a subpoena (Barsky, 2024; Reamer, 2023d). These guidelines apply to subpoenas of AI-generated data and records:

- Determine who served you with the subpoena.
- Do not release any information unless you are sure you have been authorized in writing to do so.
- Notify your employer (if applicable) so that the employer can notify the malpractice insurer.
- Notify your own malpractice insurer (to determine whether legal representation may be necessary, obtain legal advice about how to respond to the subpoena, and ensure that the insurer is notified in a timely fashion in accord with policy provisions that require the insured to notify the insurer of a potential claim). The insurance may cover the legal expense of an attorney's filing a motion to quash the subpoena or to obtain a protective order.
- Should you employ an assistant or supervise a trainee, it would be wise to claim the privilege to protect confidentiality even though the court might rule that unlicensed practitioners are not covered by the privilege.
- Determine whether the issuer of the subpoena will pay you a witness fee and cover your travel expenses.
- At a deposition where there is no judge, you might have your own attorney present or choose to follow the advice and direction of your client's attorney. Your malpractice policy may cover all or a portion of this expense.
- If you feel your information about your client is embarrassing, damaging, or immaterial, you might consider getting written permission to discuss the situation with your client's attorney.
- Unless you are required to produce records only (as with a subpoena duces tecum) and are providing all your client records (including ESI), you must appear at the location stated in the subpoena.

Practitioners can use several strategies to protect clients' confidentiality during legal proceedings that involve AI-related information (Reamer,

2023d). If practitioners believe that a subpoena is inappropriate (for example, because it requests AI-generated information that state law considers privileged), they can arrange for a lawyer (perhaps the client's lawyer) to file a *motion to quash the subpoena*, which is an attempt to have the court rule that the request contained in the subpoena is inappropriate. A judge may issue a protective order explicitly limiting the disclosure of specific privileged information during the discovery phase of the case. In addition, practitioners, perhaps through a lawyer, may request a review by the judge *in camera*—a review in the judge's chambers—of records or documents that they believe should not be disclosed in open court. The judge can then decide whether the information should be revealed in open court and made a matter of public record. Despite a local privileged communication statute and a practitioner's attempts to resist a subpoena and disclosure of confidential information generated by AI, a court could formally order the practitioner to reveal this information (Reamer, 2023d).

In a case that holds potential implications for behavioral health practitioners who use AI—*Caesar v. Mountanos* (1976)—a clinician was found in contempt of court for refusing to disclose confidential information. George Caesar, a psychiatrist, was providing treatment to Joan Seebach following injuries she allegedly sustained in an automobile accident. Despite Seebach's willingness to waive in writing the psychotherapist–patient privilege, Caesar refused to answer a number of questions concerning the relationship between Seebach's emotional condition and the accident. Caesar contended that disclosure of this confidential information could be harmful to Seebach. The United States Court of Appeals for the Ninth Circuit affirmed the judgment of the U.S. district court, concluding that there needs to be a proper balance between the conditional right of privacy encompassing the psychotherapist–patient relationship and the state's compelling need to ensure the ascertainment of the truth in court proceedings (Reamer, 2023d).

A unique challenge pertaining to behavioral health practitioners' efforts to protect confidential information shared during AI exchanges concerns the fact that some users who avail themselves of AI tools, such as chatbots, are not formal clients. Rather, some users of these AI tools are members of the general public who have not established a formal practitioner–client relationship. Thus, privileged communication statutes that provide some protection against disclosure of confidential information shared by clients with behavioral health practitioners using AI tools may not apply to members of the general public who share information with practitioners using AI tools. Behavioral health practitioners who offer AI-based services to the general public should consult with a knowledgeable attorney about the language they should use in disclaimers posted on the websites that feature AI tools concerning the confidentiality of any information provided by users, including limitations and exceptions.

Further, to protect clients, behavioral health practitioners have a duty to ensure that the AI software they are using is properly encrypted and protected from data breaches to the greatest extent possible. Practitioners must take steps to prevent inappropriate access to AI-generated data by third parties, for example, vendors who sponsor the AI software behavioral health practitioners use. According to the NASW (2021) *Code of Ethics*:

> Social workers should take reasonable steps to protect the confidentiality of electronic communications, including information provided to clients or third parties. Social workers should use applicable safeguards (such as encryption, firewalls, and passwords) when using electronic communications such as e-mail, online posts, online chat sessions, mobile communication, and text messages. (Standard 1.07[m])

Case 2.3: Marcia R. and the Subpoena

Marcia R., a social worker, provided substance use disorder counseling at an outpatient behavioral health clinic. One of her clients, who struggles with an addiction to heroin, was involved in a child custody dispute with the mother of his two young children. The attorney representing the children's mother learned through the client's answers to interrogatories in the court case (part of the discovery phase of this legal proceeding) that the father of the children had been receiving substance use disorder counseling from the social worker. The mother's attorney subpoenaed the social worker's clinical records (subpoena duces tecum), which included sensitive information generated by AI documentation software about the client's significant mental health and addiction struggles, including relapses. The social worker was concerned that disclosure of this AI-generated documentation could be used against her client in the child custody proceedings.

When Marcia was in graduate school, AI did not exist, and her professors never discussed how ESI about clients could be subpoenaed during legal proceedings. Marcia now realizes she needs to learn about the extent to which she can protect her AI-generated notes and about practical steps she can take to protect her clients' privacy.

TRANSPARENCY

Consistent with the time-honored concept of informed consent in behavioral health, practitioners who use AI should inform clients of any unauthorized disclosure of clients' PHI, for example, as a result of computer hacking or failed online or digital security (Reamer, 2023a). Practitioners have an ethical duty to be transparent with users about possible biases and misuses of AI-generated data. According to Li et al. (2023), *transparency*

> refers to the possibility of understanding an AI system's decision-making process. The black-box nature of most AI algorithms causes a lack of transparency regarding the inner reasoning of specific AI techniques, especially deep learning. In particular, the black-box's fundamental steps of analysis are opaque, as is the decision making process. These issues are exacerbated when algorithms are trained on biased data or exclude certain demographic characteristics. For instance, an AI algorithm used in the United States of America to predict accused persons' future recidivism rates showed that the risk scores for an African American with minor crimes were higher than a white American who had committed multiple crimes. Trust, public trust, patient trust, and the adoption of AI in healthcare will eventually depend on transparency. (p. 41)

According to the technology standards adopted jointly by NASW, the Association of Social Work Boards, Council on Social Work Education, and Clinical Social Work Association (2017):

> Regardless of the precautions that behavioral health practitioners take to ensure that client records are gathered, managed, and stored in a secure manner, confidential electronic records may be breached. Social workers should comply with ethical standards and relevant federal and state laws regarding any duty to inform clients about

> possible breaches of confidentiality. Social workers should also develop policies and procedures detailing how they would inform clients regarding breaches of confidentiality. (Standard 3.05)

In the United States, practitioners also have a duty to disclose any breach of AI data related to the Health Insurance Portability and Accountability Act of 1996 (HIPAA). The HIPAA Breach Notification Rule, originally published in 2000, requires HIPAA-covered entities and their business associates to provide notification following a breach of unsecured PHI. Similar breach notification provisions implemented and enforced by the Federal Trade Commission apply to vendors of personal health records and their third-party service providers, pursuant to section 13407 of the 2009 HIPAA and the Health Information Technology for Economic and Clinical Health (HITECH) Act.

A *breach*, which could involve AI-generated information, is, generally, an impermissible use or disclosure under the Privacy Rule (HIPAA, P.L. 104-191) that compromises the security or privacy of the PHI (Carter, 2025). An impermissible use or disclosure of PHI is presumed to be a breach unless the covered entity or business associate, as applicable, demonstrates that there is a low probability that the PHI has been compromised based on a risk assessment of at least the following four factors:

1. The nature and extent of the PHI involved, including the types of identifiers and the likelihood of reidentification
2. The unauthorized person who used the PHI or to whom the disclosure was made
3. Whether the PHI was actually acquired or viewed
4. The extent to which the risk to the PHI has been mitigated

Covered entities and business associates, where applicable, have discretion to provide the required breach notifications following an impermissible use or disclosure without performing a risk assessment to determine the probability that the PHI has been compromised (Carter, 2025).

Three exceptions to the definition of "breach" are relevant to AI data that include PHI (Carter, 2025; Reamer, 2023d). The first exception applies to the unintentional acquisition, access, or use of PHI by a workforce member or person acting under the authority of a covered entity or business associate if such acquisition, access, or use was made in good faith and within the scope of authority. The second exception applies to the inadvertent disclosure of PHI by a person authorized to access PHI at a covered entity or business associate to another person authorized to access PHI at the covered entity or business associate or organized healthcare arrangement in which the covered entity participates. In both cases, the information cannot be further used or disclosed in a manner not permitted by the federal Privacy Rule (HIPAA, P.L. 104-191). The third exception applies if the covered entity or business associate has a good faith belief that the unauthorized person to whom the impermissible disclosure was made would not have been able to retain the information.

Following a breach of unsecured PHI, including AI-generated data and records, covered entities must provide notification of the breach to affected individuals; the Secretary of the U.S. Department of Health and Human Services (DHHS); and, in certain circumstances, to the media. In addition, business associates must notify covered entities if a breach occurs at or by the business associate (Carter, 2025; Reamer, 2023d).

Covered entities must notify affected individuals following the discovery of a breach of unsecured PHI. Covered entities must provide this individual notice in written form by first-class mail or, alternatively, by email if the affected individual has agreed to receive such notices electronically. If the covered entity has insufficient or out-of-date contact information for 10 or more individuals, the covered entity must provide substitute individual notice by either posting the notice on the home page of its website for at least 90 days or by providing the notice in major print or broadcast media where the affected individuals likely reside. The covered entity must include a toll-free phone number that remains active for at least 90 days where individuals can learn if their information was involved in the breach. If the covered entity has insufficient or out-of-date contact information for fewer than 10 individuals, the covered entity may provide substitute notice by an alternative form of written notice, by telephone, or by other means (Carter, 2025; Reamer, 2023d).

These individual notifications must be provided without unreasonable delay and in no case later than 60 days following the discovery of a breach. The notifications must include, to the extent possible, a brief description of the breach; a description of the types of information that were involved in the breach; the steps affected individuals should take to protect themselves from potential harm; a brief description of what the covered entity is doing to investigate the breach, mitigate the harm, and prevent further breaches;

and contact information for the covered entity (or business associate, as applicable; Carter, 2025).

With respect to a breach of AI data and records at or by a business associate, while the covered entity is ultimately responsible for ensuring individuals are notified, the covered entity may delegate the responsibility of providing individual notices to the business associate (Carter, 2025; Reamer, 2023d). Covered entities and business associates should consider which entity is in the best position to provide notice to the individual, which may depend on various circumstances, such as the functions the business associate performs on behalf of the covered entity and which entity has the relationship with the individual.

Covered entities that experience a breach of AI-generated data and records affecting more than 500 residents of a state or jurisdiction are, in addition to notifying the affected individuals, required to provide notice to prominent media outlets serving the state or jurisdiction. Covered entities will likely provide this notification in the form of a press release to appropriate media outlets serving the affected area. Like individual notice, this media notification must be provided without unreasonable delay and in no case later than 60 days following the discovery of a breach and must include the same information required for the individual notice.

Case 2.4: Loretta R. and Transparency

Loretta R., a social worker, is the principal owner of a large group practice that offers a wide range of behavioral health services to adult clients. She contracted with an AI company to design and implement a chatbot that would be available to anyone who wanted emotional support and behavioral health resources related to their struggles with depression, anxiety, self-esteem, relationships, and other challenges. In addition to providing this public service, Loretta expected that some chatbot users would become clinical clients of the group practice.

To enhance transparency, Loretta sought formal consultation from a behavioral health ethics expert and an attorney who specializes in behavioral healthcare risk management to create state-of-the-art informed consent statements that would be featured prominently for any chatbot users. The informed consent statements addressed key issues related to users' privacy and confidentiality, as well as the potential benefits and risks associated with using the chatbot to seek assistance.

Loretta made the wise decision to seek ethical and legal consultation about her plans to launch chatbot support services. This exemplifies the steps that behavioral health practitioners who are considering using AI should take to protect both clients and themselves.

CLIENT MISDIAGNOSIS

Clinical behavioral health practitioners who rely on AI to assess clients' behavioral health challenges and symptoms must do their best to prevent misdiagnoses to the greatest extent possible (Reamer, 2023a). Misdiagnoses may occur when behavioral health practitioners do not supplement their AI-generated assessments with their own independent assessments and judgment or do not design protocols that ensure that users' interactions with a chatbot escalate to a human practitioner when clinically necessary. Misdiagnosis may lead to inappropriate or unwarranted clinical interventions that, in turn, may cause significant harm to clients and expose behavioral health practitioners to the risk of malpractice lawsuits and licensing board complaints (Reamer, 2023a, 2023b). According to Yan et al. (2023), "Current AI is still far from effectively recognizing mental disorders and cannot replace clinicians' diagnoses in the near future" (p. 2).

Several studies have explored the accuracy of mental health diagnoses using AI tools. For example, researchers at the French Institute for Research in Computer Science and Automation used "proxy measures" for mental health and found that AI provided an accurate diagnosis up to about 90 percent of the time (Dunleavy, 2021). The researchers used information for more than 500,000 adults from the UK Biobank, a database of medical reports and questionnaire responses gauging personal statistics and behaviors.

In another study, Abd-alrazaq et al. (2022) identified 15 systematic reviews of 852 studies of the ability of AI tools to diagnose Alzheimer's disease, mild cognitive impairment, schizophrenia, bipolar disorder, autism spectrum disorder, obsessive–compulsive disorder, PTSD, and psychotic disorders. The accuracy of AI models in diagnosing these mental disorders ranged between 21 percent and 100 percent. According to Bateman (2021):

> Utilizing AI technology, therapists can sift through large amounts of data to identify family histories, patient behaviours and responses to prior treatments, to make a more precise diagnosis and to make more insightful decisions about treatment and choice of therapist.

Case 2.5: Juanita G. and AI in Client Diagnosis

Juanita G., a mental health counselor in a large mental health center, oversaw the development of a chatbot that provided users—most of whom were not clients of the agency—with information about symptoms of mental illness, treatment options, and resources. The chatbot posed a series of automated questions to users that it used to provide tentative diagnoses (the chatbot's introductory statement made it clear that these were possible diagnoses that needed to be verified by trained professionals). An attorney who was retained by the mental health center cautioned the mental health counselor about possible liability risks associated with potential misdiagnoses. They worked together to craft a very carefully worded disclaimer about the tentativeness of the chatbot-generated diagnosis.

Juanita wisely recognized that her use of AI to provide users with information about symptoms and treatment exposes her to some legal risk, especially if the AI tool provides any misleading or inaccurate information to users. In comparable situations, behavioral health practitioners can take several steps to protect clients and themselves. In addition to obtaining legal consultation, practitioners should also review relevant ethical and practice-based standards related to the use of AI for clinical purposes.

CLIENT ABANDONMENT

Behavioral health practitioners who rely on AI to connect with clients must take steps to respond to their messages and postings in a timely fashion—when that is a possibility with the software—and advise clients of the limitations of AI during crises. To use the legal term, behavioral health practitioners must take steps to avoid "abandoning" clients who use AI to communicate significant distress. In malpractice litigation, *abandonment* occurs when practitioners do not respond to clients in a timely fashion or terminate services in a manner inconsistent with standards in the profession (Reamer, 2023d). For example, a client who communicates suicidal ideation via AI, does not receive a timely response from their clinician, and attempts to die by suicide yet lives may have grounds for a malpractice claim. According to the NASW (2021) *Code of Ethics*:

> Social workers should take reasonable steps to avoid abandoning clients who are still in need of services. Social workers should withdraw services precipitously only under unusual circumstances, giving careful consideration to all factors in the situation and taking care to minimize possible adverse effects. Social workers should assist in making appropriate arrangements for continuation of services when necessary. (Standard 1.17[b])

Similarly, the American Association for Marriage and Family Therapy (AAMFT, 2015) code states, "Marriage and family therapists do not abandon or neglect clients in treatment without making reasonable arrangements for the continuation of treatment" (Standard 1.11). The American Counseling Association (ACA, 2014) code states, "Counselors do not abandon or neglect clients in counseling" (Standard A.12).

Case 2.6: Vicky M. and Client Abandonment

Vicky M., a mental health counselor, created a chatbot for current clients that enabled them to get information about the behavioral health challenges they face, self-care techniques, and resources. One client used the chatbot to request crisis services. This client was experiencing suicidal thoughts and thought they could use the chatbot to request emergency services. The counselor neglected to include a clear disclaimer advising users to not use the chatbot for crisis or emergency services. The client became distraught when they did not get an immediate response from their clinician and attempted suicide. The client survived the suicide attempt and subsequently filed a lawsuit and licensing board complaint against the counselor, alleging abandonment. The client, who admitted that they did not fully understand the nature and limitations of chatbots, claimed that they had no reason to believe they could not use the mental health counselor's chatbot to seek assistance in a crisis.

Unfortunately, when Vicky created and implemented her chatbot tool, she was not familiar with practical risk management steps behavioral health practitioners who use AI can take to protect clients and themselves. Had she reviewed relevant risk management protocols in advance and sought consultation from ethics and legal experts, Vicky may have been able to prevent the client's suicide attempt and the subsequent lawsuit and licensing board complaint.

CLIENT SURVEILLANCE

One of the inherent risks of AI is the possibility that third parties will use available data inappropriately and without authorization for surveillance purposes. For example, behavioral health practitioners who provide reproductive health services to clients in states where abortion is illegal must be cognizant of the possibility that prosecutors will subpoena ESI generated by AI to prosecute pregnant people who seek abortion services and the practitioners who assist them in their decision making (Reamer, 2023b). Although ESI in behavioral health practitioners' possession has always been discoverable during legal proceedings, there is a newer challenge when ESI includes information generated by AI (for example, information about reproductive health generated by chatbots used by clients and behavioral health practitioners). A client or practitioner who uses AI to search online for abortion-related information services creates a digital trail (Reamer, 2023b).

According to the Federal Rules of Civil Procedure (Yeazell et al., 2022), *ESI* is defined as any documents or information that is stored in electronic form. According to Rule 34 of the Federal Rules of Civil Procedure, a party may serve on any other party a request to produce and permit the requesting party or its representative to inspect, copy, test, or sample any designated documents or ESI stored in any medium from which information can be obtained either directly or, if necessary, after translation by the responding party into a reasonably usable form (Yeazell et al., 2022). Rule 34 applies to electronic data compilations from which information can be obtained only with the use of detection devices and that when the data can, as a practical matter, be made usable by the discovering party only through respondent's devices, the respondent may be required to use their devices to translate the data into usable form. In many instances, this means that a respondent will have to supply a printout of computer data.

States have adopted similar rules governing legal proceedings in state courts (Reamer, 2023d). These rules provide attorneys with guidelines related to subpoenaing ESI, which, in theory, might be used against clients and practitioners who use AI tools.

Case 2.7: Belinda F. and Client Surveillance

Belinda F., a social worker, provides counseling services at a women's health clinic. A new patient at the clinic told Belinda that she was pregnant as a result of a sexual assault. The patient handed Belinda a copy of an online news article about the alleged perpetrator's recent arrest for rape. The patient explained that she had met the man at a friend's party and that the man had spiked her alcoholic drink with GHB (gamma-hydroxybutyric acid), commonly known as a date-rape drug.

The clinic patient told Belinda that she had decided to terminate the pregnancy because of the emotional trauma associated with the sexual assault. The patient acknowledged that state law prohibits abortion; she asked Belinda to help her locate the nearest state that permits abortion and find resources to help with travel expenses.

The electronic health record Belinda uses includes an AI feature that enables staffers to record clinical sessions—with patients' consent—upload the recording to the AI platform, and use the AI platform to generate the clinical note. Belinda was concerned about the possibility that this recording and AI-generated note would provide evidence that the patient and she had discussed abortion options, which might expose them to the risk of criminal prosecution under state law.

When Belinda started her social work career, she used paper records to document clinical encounters. In contrast, Belinda's current employer expects her to rely on AI software to generate her clinical notes. Belinda has never received training on the ethical implications of this protocol, including the possibility that her notes could be used against her clients and herself. She recognized she needed to learn about these risks and steps she can take to protect clients and herself.

PLAGIARISM, DISHONESTY, FRAUD, DECEPTION, AND MISREPRESENTATION

One advantage of AI is that it enables behavioral health practitioners to generate useful job-related information quickly. For example, behavioral health practitioners may use AI for administrative tasks, for example, to produce content that may be useful in grant applications, project summaries, program evaluations, advocacy efforts, and fundraising appeals. Behavioral health practitioners who rely on content produced by AI tools must be sure to cite their sources and comply with "fair use" doctrine to avoid allegations of plagiarism, dishonesty, fraud, and misrepresentation (Keegan, 2023; Reamer, 2023a).

Although the populating of reports, applications, and other documents with content generated by AI tools is not necessarily plagiarism, it is possible that these tools incorporate content from other authors whose work should be cited (Pocock, 2024). Behavioral health practitioners who use AI should comply with prevailing ethical standards (Reamer, 2023c). For example, the NASW (2021) *Code of Ethics* states:

> Social workers should not participate in, condone, or be associated with dishonesty, fraud, or deception. (Standard 4.04)
>
> Social workers should take responsibility and credit, including authorship credit, only for work they have actually performed and to which they have contributed. (Standard 4.08[a])
>
> Social workers should honestly acknowledge the work of and the contributions made by others. (Standard 4.08[b])

Similarly, the APA (2017) code of conduct states, "Psychologists do not present portions of another's work or data as their own, even if the other work or data source is cited occasionally" (Standard 8.11).

The risk of deception can arise in other contexts as well when behavioral health practitioners use AI. For example, as discussed earlier, social robots can provide emotional support, companionship, and personal assistance services to older adults, people with disabilities, children with special needs, and other vulnerable populations (Formosa, 2021). Social robots are developed using AI and are often equipped with sensors, cameras, microphones, and other technology so they can respond to touch, sounds, and visual cues much like humans would. Using AI, robots can decipher facial expressions, engage in conversations, respond with a smile, read emails, place video calls, tell stories and jokes, and track humans with their eyes to prove they are paying attention (Robinson & Kavanagh, 2021). As a result of cognitive impairment or other challenges, some clients may not fully understand that they are not interacting with a human being.

Case 2.8: Katarina S. and Plagiarism

Katarina S., a marriage and family therapist, serves as the clinical director of an outpatient behavioral health clinic. Katarina was responsible for preparing and submitting an application for grant funds that would be used to develop and implement a treatment program for high-risk clients who struggle with co-occurring behavioral health symptoms (for example, substance use disorder and psychiatric symptoms). Because she was juggling several time-consuming tasks, Katarina was concerned that she might be unable to submit the grant application by the strict deadline.

One section of the grant application needed to include a comprehensive discussion of state-of-the-art professional literature on evidence-based treatment of co-occurring issues. To save time, Katarina accessed a popular AI tool that provides detailed information in response to users' queries. She asked the chatbot for a summary of peer-reviewed literature on evidence-based treatment of co-occurring issues. She then copied and pasted significant portions of the chatbot's results into the grant application draft without citing the source of this information.

Katarina's wish to use AI to save time when she prepared the grant application is certainly understandable. Many behavioral health administrators find that there are not enough hours in the day to complete the tasks on their to-do lists. However, Katarina violated ethical standards and faced legal risk when she used AI to generate content for the grant application and inserted it in the document without editing and proper citation and attribution.

ALGORITHMIC BIAS AND UNFAIRNESS

AI's dependence on ML, which draws from large volumes of data obtained from samples that may not be entirely representative of behavioral health practitioners' clients, may lead to what is known as *algorithmic bias*. AI-based algorithms used to assess clients and develop interventions and treatment plans may incorporate significant bias related to race, ethnicity, socioeconomic status (SES), gender, sexual orientation, gender expression, and other protected categories if the samples on which these algorithms depend are not truly representative (Reamer, 2023a; Trail, 2024). Algorithmic bias can also manifest itself when AI is used as part of a behavioral healthcare agency's tools, including employee recruitment, online marketing, and facial recognition protocol. According to Lee et al. (2019):

> Because machines can treat similarly situated people and objects differently, research is starting to reveal some troubling examples in

> which the reality of algorithmic decision making falls short of our expectations. Given this, some algorithms run the risk of replicating and even amplifying human biases, particularly those affecting protected groups. (para. 4)

In behavioral health, bias can be caused by self-learning algorithms implemented during the self-learning process. It can come from sampling bias that generates systematic error or an unintended tendency of AI algorithms to prefer one outcome over another (Li et al., 2023).

In a major study, Julian Nyarko and colleagues at the Stanford University Human-Centered Artificial Intelligence project explored whether there is evidence of ethnic bias in the use of large language models, such as ChatGPT (Schreiber, 2024). This creative research focused on five scenarios in which a user might seek advice using AI: (1) strategies for purchasing an item like a car or bicycle, which were designed to assess bias in the area of SES; (2) questions about likely outcomes in chess, which assessed bias related to intellectual capabilities; (3) queries about who might be more likely to win public office, which is about electability and popularity; (4) sports ability; and (5) advice-seeking in connection with making a job offer to someone. Indeed, the authors found noteworthy evidence of systemic bias based on these prompts:

> This is a little bit like a game of Whac-a-Mole, where issues have to be fixed piece-by-piece as they are discovered. Overall, how to debias models is still a very active and exploratory field of research.
>
> That said, at a minimum, I think we should know that these biases exist, and companies who deploy LLMs should test for these biases. (Schreiber, 2024, paras. 1 and 2 following the question, "Which leads to the question of what should be done . . . ?")

Behavioral health codes of ethics implore practitioners to avoid discrimination. For example, NAADAC, The Association for Addiction Professionals (NAADAC, 2021) *Code of Ethics* states, "Providers shall not use cultural or values differences as a reason to engage in discrimination" (Standard IV-4). The APA (2017) code states, "In their work-related activities, psychologists do not engage in unfair discrimination based on age, gender, gender identity, race, ethnicity, culture, national origin, religion, sexual orientation, disability, SES, or any basis proscribed by law" (Standard 3.01). The NASW (2021) *Code of Ethics* states:

> Social workers should not practice, condone, facilitate, or collaborate with any form of discrimination on the basis of race, ethnicity, national origin, color, sex, sexual orientation, gender identity or expression, age, marital status, political belief, religion, immigration status, or mental or physical ability. (Standard 4.02)

Case 2.9: Audrey K. and Algorithmic Bias

Audrey K., a psychiatrist, is the medical director of an outpatient clinic associated with a psychiatric hospital. The clinic serves a culturally diverse patient population in a large lower income community. Audrey has enjoyed studying state-of-the-art online and digital technologies that can be used in the treatment of psychiatric disorders. At a professional conference, she learned about an innovative AI tool that patients can access with questions about management of their symptoms to support their treatment.

Audrey asked the representative of the AI tool's developer, who featured the product in the conference's exhibit hall, about the large language model database that the company uses to generate responses to users' queries. She was especially interested in knowing whether the AI tool's database includes significant numbers of culturally diverse, low-income patients whose understanding and beliefs about the treatment of mental illness may be unique. The company representative said they did not have this information and would have to "look into it" and get back to Audrey.

Kudos to Audrey. She recognized that the databases on which AI behavioral health tools depend may incorporate some bias. This is especially problematic when AI tools draw on clinical samples that do not reflect the demographic attributes of behavioral health professionals' clientele.

CONCLUSION

In this chapter, I provided an overview of ethical issues related to informed consent and client autonomy; privacy and confidentiality; transparency; client misdiagnosis; client abandonment; client surveillance; plagiarism, dishonesty, fraud, and misrepresentation; and algorithmic bias and unfairness. I now turn to a discussion of "best practices" designed to ensure ethical use of AI in the behavioral health professions.

3

Best Practices in the Use of Artificial Intelligence in Behavioral Health

Behavioral health practitioners who use AI have an ethical responsibility to comply with prevailing "best practice" standards that draw on the best available empirical evidence. For example, the NASW (2021) *Code of Ethics* states:

> Social workers should strive to become and remain proficient in professional practice and the performance of professional functions. Social workers should critically examine and keep current with emerging knowledge relevant to social work. Social workers should routinely review the professional literature and participate in continuing education relevant to social work practice and social work ethics. (Standard 4.01[b])
>
> Social workers should base practice on recognized knowledge, including empirically based knowledge, relevant to social work and social work ethics. (Standard 4.01[c])
>
> Social workers should critically examine and keep current with emerging knowledge relevant to social work and fully use evaluation and research evidence in their professional practice. (Standard 5.02[c])

Ethical standards related directly to behavioral health practitioners' use of AI are evolving. As Li et al. (2023) noted:

> In modern life, the application of artificial intelligence (AI) has promoted the implementation of data-driven algorithms in high-stakes

> domains, such as healthcare. However, it is becoming increasingly challenging for humans to understand the working and reasoning of these complex and opaque algorithms. For AI to support essential decisions in these domains, specific ethical issues need to be addressed to prevent the misinterpretation of AI, which may have severe consequences for humans. (p. 28)

In this chapter, I discuss "best practices" designed to ensure ethical use of AI in the behavioral health professions. Key topics are drawing on core ethics concepts, creating ethics-based governing principles, establishing a digital ethics steering committee, convening diverse focus groups, subjecting algorithms to peer review, conducting AI simulations, developing clinician-focused guidance for interpreting AI results, developing rigorous communication and training protocols, maintaining a log of AI results to identify positive and negative trends, testing algorithms for possible biases and inaccuracies, and continuously monitoring algorithmic decision processes (Gattadahalli, 2020; Li et al., 2023; Reamer, 2023a).

UNDERSTANDING CORE ETHICS CONCEPTS—THE ROOTS OF BEST PRACTICES

Ethics-informed guidelines for the use of AI by behavioral health professionals have been influenced by widely accepted moral concepts first established with the advent of the field of professional ethics in the 1970s. The biomedical ethicists Tom Beauchamp and James Childress (2019) developed the best-known framework for understanding professionals' virtues in the 1970s, when the fields of biomedical ethics and professional ethics were just emerging and gaining prominence. This prominent framework, first published in 1979 (Beauchamp & Childress, 1979), continues to be central to the professional ethics field and is highly relevant to the use of AI in behavioral health. Beauchamp and Childress identified several core, or "focal," virtues that are critically important in the work carried out by professionals and can provide a valuable guide to the development of AI-related best practices.

Compassion

Compassion is central to behavioral healthcare. Its key elements include having deep empathy for those who struggle in life and having concern about their suffering. Behavioral health professionals who use AI should do so primarily because of the ways in which AI tools can enhance the practitioners' ability to care for the people they serve.

Discernment

The virtue of *discernment* involves the ability to make judgments and reach decisions without being unduly influenced by extraneous or irrelevant factors, such as personal bias, relationships, or political or religious ideology. Behavioral health practitioners who use AI should exercise keen, thoughtful judgment about the ways in which it can be used ethically.

Trustworthiness

Trust entails a belief that one can rely on the moral character and competence of another person. To trust someone—to know they have the attribute of *trustworthiness*—is to believe that this individual will act ethically and with the right motives. Behavioral health practitioners who use AI should seek to enhance users' (both clients' and the general public's) confidence that practitioners are using these tools responsibly and in users' best interests.

Integrity

A person who has *integrity* is truthful, honest, and acts in accordance with core moral values. Behavioral health practitioners who use AI should do so with utmost integrity consistent with prevailing ethical standards in the behavioral health professions.

Conscientiousness

An individual with the trait of *conscientiousness* is motivated to do what is right because it is right. Behavioral health practitioners who use AI should do so conscientiously and with overriding concern about protection of users' rights.

These five focal virtues are linked directly to four core moral principles that Beauchamp and Childress (2019) claimed constitute the moral foundation of professional practice: (1) autonomy, (2) nonmaleficence, (3) beneficence, and (4) justice. These oft-cited moral principles clearly have broad application to, and implications for, the use of AI in behavioral health.

Autonomy

The concept of *autonomy*—which is closely connected with the enduring behavioral healthcare value of client self-determination—implies that people have the right to decide what is best for them—free from coercion. An autonomous individual (for example, a client who chooses to use AI to enhance the quality of their life) acts freely in accordance with their wishes and preferences. A client who struggles with cognitive impairment may be at risk of being controlled by AI. Behavioral health practitioners should assess potential AI users' ability to make sound and informed decisions and should not use any form of coercion with respect to the use of AI.

Nonmaleficence

The principle of *nonmaleficence* assumes that people will not knowingly harm others. Typical examples include not killing; not causing pain or suffering; not incapacitating; not being racist or homophobic; not manipulating or coercing; and not depriving others of food, housing, and healthcare. Thus, behavioral health practitioners should not use AI in ways that can harm their clients.

Beneficence

The principle of *beneficence* entails acts of mercy, kindness, and altruism to benefit others. Behavioral health practitioners' actions typically are rooted in beneficence; thus, they should use AI only when there is evidence that doing so will benefit users.

Justice

The principle of *justice* entails behaving in a way that is fair, equitable, appropriate, and respectful of people's rights. An *injustice* thus involves a wrongful act or omission that harms people. Behavioral health practitioners are especially concerned about promoting justice among people who are vulnerable (for example, frail older adults, neglected children), oppressed (for example, victims of racial, ethnic, or social discrimination), or living in poverty. Practitioners should aim to use AI in ways that enhance their ability to promote social justice and challenge social injustice. Practitioners must be steadfast in their efforts to avoid the use of AI that is susceptible to algorithmic bias.

Case 3.1: Bahwani M. and AI Governing Principles

Bahwani M., a clinical psychologist, is a clinical director at a large group practice that employs psychologists, social workers, mental health counselors, substance use disorder treatment professionals, and a psychiatric nurse. Bahwani met with a vendor who promoted an AI tool that would enable the practice's clinicians to record counseling sessions, upload the recordings to the AI company's platform, and use the AI technology to generate session notes for clients' electronic records.

Bahwani presented the AI documentation tool to her colleagues, who agreed that this was an appealing option that would save the group's staffers significant time during a typical workday. She informed her colleagues that the group would need to spend substantial time identifying ethical and risk management challenges associated with the use of this AI tool and develop policies and protocols to protect clients and the practitioners.

CREATING ETHICS-BASED GOVERNING PRINCIPLES

AI initiatives should adhere to prominent ethics-informed principles to ensure these efforts are designed and implemented responsibly (Gattadahalli, 2020; Li et al., 2023; Reamer, 2023a). Key principles include the following:

The AI technology does no harm. AI developers should take steps to protect clients and other members of the public they serve. For example, in Case 3.1, the group practice that considered adopting the AI documentation tool must ensure that sharing recordings of clinical sessions does not violate clients' privacy rights. This group of clinicians should investigate the AI company's privacy protection protocols, including compliance with relevant federal laws (which in the United States, for example, includes the HIPAA of 1996 and the 2017 Title 42 CFR Part 2), state laws, and code of ethics standards.

The AI technology is designed and developed using transparent protocols and auditable methodologies. Referring to the clinical group in Case 3.1, the group should prepare clearly worded and transparent disclosure statements that inform clients and potential clients about their use of the AI documentation tool and any risks associated with it. The group should also take steps to monitor this AI tool to ensure there are no privacy breaches. As Li et al. (2023) noted, "Explainability is essential to responsible AI and can build trust in and engagement with AI" (p. 29).

AI tools collect and treat client data to reduce biases against population groups based on race, ethnicity, culture, gender, sexual orientation, gender expression, religion, and other potential sources

of bias. The clinical group (see Case 3.1) should confer with the AI company's representatives regarding the steps they have taken, if any, to prevent algorithmic bias in the tool's documentation protocol. This is especially important given this clinical group's clientele, which is diverse with respect to race, ethnicity, culture, gender, sexual orientation, gender expression, religion, and primary language.

Clients are informed of known risks and benefits of AI technologies so they can make informed decisions about its use. Referring to Case 3.1, the primary beneficiaries of this AI tool would be the group's clinicians, who, in theory, would save time associated with documentation of their clinical services. The clinical group would be ethically obligated to inform all clients about their use of the AI tool, including any possible risks—no matter how remote—especially related to possible privacy breaches and unauthorized access.

Case 3.2: Bryan M. and the AI Ethics Steering Committee

Bryan M., the clinical director of a substance use disorders treatment program, contracted with an AI company to provide all clients with wearable sensors and smartphone apps they can use to monitor key physiological parameters associated with behavioral health challenges (for example, heart rate, breathing patterns) and behavioral parameters (for example, sleep quality, physical activity, social interactions); provide real-time feedback (for example, stress and anxiety patterns); and provide personalized interventions (for example, ways to reduce anxiety and enhance sleep). The program's board of directors, which approved the contract with the AI company, instructed the clinical director to create a committee that would monitor the design and implementation of this AI tool.

ESTABLISHING A DIGITAL ETHICS STEERING COMMITTEE

Ideally, organizations that employ behavioral health practitioners and use AI would create a digital ethics steering committee comprising key staff who are familiar with digital technology in general, AI technology, and prevailing ethical standards and best practices (Gattadahalli, 2020; Reamer, 2023a).

In Case 3.2 presented earlier, Bryan M.'s committee would have oversight responsibilities related to the design and implementation of AI. This effort is consistent with prominent code of ethics standards in behavioral health. For example, the NASW (2021) *Code of Ethics* states:

> With growth in the use of communication technology in various aspects of social work practice, social workers need to be aware of the unique challenges that may arise in relation to the maintenance of confidentiality, informed consent, professional boundaries, professional competence, record keeping, and other ethical considerations. (Purpose, para. 10)

CONVENING DIVERSE FOCUS GROUPS

Focus groups that include individuals from the diverse populations from whom datasets used in AI may be collected can help reduce and prevent algorithmic bias. Focus groups may include clients, client advocates, practitioners, researchers, educators, community leaders, agency administrators, and policymakers (Gattadahalli, 2020; Reamer, 2023a). They can review current AI protocols and suggest modifications to address risks related to algorithmic bias. This effort is consistent with code of ethics standards in behavioral health. For example, the NAADAC (2021) *Code of Ethics* states:

> Addiction professionals shall be knowledgeable and aware of diverse cultural, individual, societal, and role differences amongst the clients they serve in a diversity of settings along the continuum of care. Providers shall offer services that demonstrate appropriate respect for the fundamental rights, dignity and worth of all clients. (Standard IV-1)

The ACA (2014) *Code of Ethics* states, "Counselors recognize that culture affects the manner in which clients' problems are defined and experienced. Clients' socioeconomic and cultural experiences are considered when diagnosing mental disorders" (Standard E.5.b).

Case 3.3: Jorge G. and the AI Focus Group

A mental health agency received a large foundation grant to design a chatbot that community members could use to obtain information and resource suggestions related to a wide range of behavioral health challenges. The agency serves a culturally diverse community with varied views about the nature of mental illness and culturally acceptable interventions (including the use of psychotropic and neuroleptic medication, homeopathic remedies, psychiatric hospitalization, faith-based healers, and counseling). Jorge G., the chair of the agency's board of directors, recognized the need to convene a cross-section of community members to get their feedback on the chatbot's goals and design and to discuss ways to be sensitive to the reactions of potential users whose racial, ethnic, linguistic, and other cultural backgrounds might influence the way they engage with the chatbot.

SUBJECTING ALGORITHMS TO PEER REVIEW

Rigorous peer review processes can help identify and address blind spots and weaknesses in AI protocols. Peer reviewers may include behavioral health practitioners familiar with AI, researchers, educators, and diverse groups of data scientists (Gattadahalli, 2020; Reamer, 2023a). This effort is consistent with code of ethics standards in behavioral health. For example, the NASW (2021) *Code of Ethics* states, "Social workers should seek the advice and counsel of colleagues whenever such consultation is in the best interests of clients" (Standard 2.05[a]).

Case 3.4: Lucy F. and the Peer Advisory Group

Lucy F., the director of behavioral health for an urban school district, was eager to expand high school students' access to behavioral health resources. She was especially concerned about long waiting lists in this community for counseling services and that many students' families lack comprehensive insurance coverage for behavioral health services.

Lucy consulted with an AI company about developing a chatbot that would provide high school students with behavioral health resources in the event of a crisis or more chronic concerns (including contact information for local professional services, relevant websites, and self-help literature). She convened an advisory group of seasoned behavioral health practitioners and academicians who specialize in the treatment of high-risk adolescents to discuss best practices associated with chatbots and to review and test *beta versions*—early or testing versions that can be evaluated and modified before being released to the public—of the chatbot.

CONDUCTING AI SIMULATIONS

To reduce risk and address possible bias, it can be useful to develop simulation models that test scenarios in which AI tools are susceptible to algorithmic bias. Feedback generated by simulations can identify potential ethics-related problems associated with AI (Gattadahalli, 2020; Reamer, 2023a). This effort is consistent with code of ethics standards in behavioral health. For example, the ACA (2014) *Code of Ethics* states, "Counselors continually monitor their effectiveness as professionals and take steps to improve when necessary. Counselors take reasonable steps to seek peer supervision to evaluate their efficacy as counselors" (Standard C.2.d). The NASW (2021) *Code of Ethics* states, "Social workers should monitor and evaluate policies, the implementation of programs, and practice interventions" (Standard 5.02[a]).

A research group at the Brookings Institution identified algorithmic bias risks associated with AI and strategies to address them (Lee et al., 2019). The group proposed a framework to enhance "algorithmic hygiene," which identifies some specific causes of biases and employs best practices to identify and mitigate them. The group highlighted risks associated with bias in online job recruitment tools, word associations, online ads, facial recognition technology, and criminal justice protocols. Their report included several proposals to mitigate algorithmic bias:

- Nondiscrimination and other civil rights laws should be updated to interpret and redress online disparate effects. Ideally, AI developers can clarify how these nondiscrimination laws apply to the types of grievances embedded in AI.
- Operators of algorithms must develop a *bias impact statement*, which can help probe and avert any potential biases that are built into or result from an algorithmic decision. As a best practice, operators of algorithms should brainstorm a core set of initial assumptions about the algorithm's purpose before its development and implementation. The bias impact statement can be based on answers to key questions that are relevant to behavioral healthcare providers:
    - Who is the audience for the algorithm, and who will be most affected by it?
    - Do we have training data to make the correct predictions about the decision?

- Are the training data sufficiently diverse and reliable?
- What is the data lifecycle of the algorithm?
- Which groups are we worried about when it comes to training data errors, disparate treatment, and effects?
- How and when will the algorithm be tested?
- Who will be the targets for testing?
- What will be the threshold for measuring and correcting for bias in the algorithm, especially as it relates to protected groups?
- What will we gain in the development of the algorithm?
- What are the potential bad outcomes, and how will we know?
- How open will we make the design process of the algorithm to internal partners, clients, and customers?
- What intervention will be taken if we predict that there might be bad outcomes associated with the development or deployment of the algorithm?
- What is the feedback loop for the algorithm for developers, internal partners, and customers?
- Is there a role for public organizations in the design of the algorithm?
- Will the algorithm have implications for cultural groups and play out differently in cultural contexts?
- Is the design team representative enough to capture these nuances and predict the application of the algorithm within different cultural contexts? If not, what steps are being taken to make these scenarios more salient and understandable to designers?
- Given the algorithm's purpose, are the training data sufficiently diverse?
- Are there statutory guardrails that companies should be reviewing to ensure that the algorithm is both legal and ethical?

- Operators of algorithms should regularly audit for bias. Facial recognition software that misidentifies persons of color more than White people is an instance in which a stakeholder or user can spot biased outcomes without knowing anything about how the algorithm makes decisions.
- The design and monitoring of algorithms should include increased human involvement. People will continue to play a role in identifying

and correcting biased outcomes long after an algorithm is developed, tested, and launched. Although more data can inform automated decision making, this process should complement rather than fully replace human judgment.

Case 3.5: Maria D. and Algorithmic Bias

Maria D., a psychiatrist at a residential treatment program, coordinates clinical supervision for behavioral health clinicians. The clinicians represent diverse racial, ethnic, linguistic, sexual orientation, gender expression, religious, and other cultural groups. Her duties include monitoring the quality of clinical services, conducting quality assessments, providing clinicians with feedback on their clinical skills, and arranging staff development training.

Maria learned about an AI platform that creates customized AI algorithms for each behavioral health setting that uses that platform to provide training and supervision of clinical staffers. The platform automatically generates "quality" metrics from a recording or transcript of clinical sessions. Those metrics provide clinicians and supervisors with reports of clinicians' use of talk time, therapeutic skills proficiency, empathy, engagement skills, reflective listening, use of open and closed questions, and collaboration skills. This psychiatrist recognized the importance of running multiple simulations before implementing the AI platform formally to ensure its validity and to assess for any algorithmic bias.

DEVELOPING CLINICIAN-FOCUSED GUIDANCE FOR INTERPRETING AI RESULTS

Behavioral health practitioners must be trained to give appropriate weight to AI tools to supplement—and not replace—their professional judgment. It is essential that practitioners understand distinctions between appropriate and inappropriate use of AI. This effort is consistent with code of ethics standards in behavioral health. For example, the NASW (2021) *Code of Ethics* states:

> Social workers who use technology in the provision of social work services should ensure that they have the necessary knowledge and skills to provide such services in a competent manner. This includes

> an understanding of the special communication challenges when using technology and the ability to implement strategies to address these challenges. (Standard 1.04[d])

The ACA (2014) *Code of Ethics* states, "Counselors who engage in the use of distance counseling, technology, and/or social media develop knowledge and skills regarding related technical, ethical, and legal considerations" (Standard H.1.a).

Case 3.6: Miremba K. and AI Clinical Guidance

The faculty of an MSW program at a local university agreed that its students need to learn about the ways in which AI is being used in the profession and about emerging ethical standards. One of the professors, Miremba K., chairs a committee that drafted content to include in a curriculum module, which would be taught to all of the MSW program's students. A key component of the module focuses on the role of AI-generated information when social workers make clinical judgments and the relationship between this information and information practitioners obtain during their direct encounters with clients.

DEVELOPING RIGOROUS COMMUNICATION AND TRAINING PROTOCOLS

As applications of AI in behavioral healthcare evolve, creating a carefully designed messaging strategy is important to ensure that the key benefits and risks of AI will be understood by clients and practitioners and can be clearly and coherently communicated to clients by their practitioners. Developing an effective communication and training protocol is essential (Gattadahalli, 2020; Reamer, 2023a). This effort is consistent with code of ethics standards in behavioral health. For example, the AAMFT (2015) *Code of Ethics* states, "Marriage and family therapists ensure that they are well trained and competent in the use of all chosen technology-assisted professional services" (Standard 6.6). The ACA (2014) *Code of Ethics* states, "Counselors practice in specialty areas new to them only after appropriate education, training, and supervised experience. While developing skills in new specialty areas, counselors take steps to ensure the competence of their work and protect others from possible harm" (Standard C.2.b).

Case 3.7: Megan K. and AI Training Protocols

Megan K., a mental health counselor, is the director of training and staff development at an agency that serves older adults and people with disabilities. The agency's board of directors recently approved the use of social robots that use AI to provide clients with companionship and to assist them with some activities of daily living. Megan recognized that most staffers were unfamiliar with this technology or the potential benefits and challenges associated with social robots.

Megan prepared a detailed user's manual that summarizes logistical steps and protocols for agency staffers' use of social robots, and she scheduled a series of in-service trainings. She recognized that these time-consuming tasks were necessary to protect clients and staffers and to ensure compliance with prevailing ethics standards.

MAINTAINING A LOG OF AI RESULTS

Ideally, organizations that employ behavioral health practitioners and use AI will maintain a comprehensive database that summarizes the results of periodic tests to identify the strengths and limitations of their AI protocols. Over time, this database can be monitored to enhance the effectiveness of AI and compliance with relevant ethical standards (Gattadahalli, 2020; Reamer, 2023a). This effort is consistent with code of ethics standards in behavioral health. For example, the ACA (2014) *Code of Ethics* states, "Counselors continually monitor their effectiveness as professionals and take steps to improve when necessary" (Standard C.2.d). The NASW (2021) *Code of Ethics* states, "Social workers should monitor and evaluate policies, the implementation of programs, and practice interventions" (Standard 5.02[a]).

Case 3.8: David S. and the Chatbot Log

David S., a marriage and family therapist, is the education director at a post-graduate training institute that certifies clinicians. The institute provides free or low-cost counseling to community members by clinicians enrolled in the institute who use these sessions as supervised training opportunities.

The institute provides its students with training in the use of chatbots. It also offers clients who receive services from trainees the opportunity to use a chatbot to receive advice about management of challenges they face and to obtain a wide range of self-help resources. David consulted with an AI expert to create a log of the chatbot's results and practical steps to monitor the pattern of users' queries and assess the quality of the chatbot's responses. David shared these data regularly with the institute's staff and students.

TESTING ALGORITHMS

Rigorous testing, ideally complemented by randomized controlled experiments that assess the effect of AI tools, is an effective method of isolating and reducing or eliminating sources of bias (Gattadahalli, 2020; Reamer, 2023a). The principal advantage of randomized trials is that this is the most effective way to control for extraneous factors (for example, students' access to other services outside the university counseling center, the effect of students' maturation) that might account for differences in outcome between two randomly assigned groups of people. This effort is consistent with code of ethics standards in behavioral health. For example, the APA (2017) code of conduct says, "Psychologists' work is based upon established scientific and professional knowledge of the discipline" (Standard 2.04). The NASW (2021) *Code of Ethics* states, "Social workers should base practice on recognized knowledge, including empirically based knowledge, relevant to social work and social work ethics" (Standard 4.01[c]).

Case 3.9: Jenn M. and Testing Algorithms

Jenn M., a clinical psychologist, serves as the clinical director of a university counseling center. They supervised implementation of a chatbot that students could access to provide them with both information about mental health challenges they experience and helpful resources. Jenn designed a study that would assess the effect of the chatbot. The study, approved by the university's institutional review board, randomly assigned a sample of university students to two groups. Students in one group were provided access to the chatbot; students in the second group were not.

At the outset of the study, all of the students were invited to complete an online comprehensive assessment of their current mental health using a well-known standardized psychometric instrument, including details about any challenging symptoms they were experiencing. Four months later, the standardized instrument was readministered to all of the students. The researchers also gathered data about the extent to which the students availed themselves of the chatbot resource or in-person counseling. Statistical analysis explored whether there were statistically significant differences between the mental health status of the two groups.

MONITORING ALGORITHMIC DECISION PROCESSES

AI, by its nature, is always evolving; consequently, algorithmic decision processes must be monitored, assessed, and refined continuously (Gattadahalli, 2020; Reamer, 2023a). This effort is consistent with code of ethics standards in behavioral health. For example, the NASW (2021) *Code of Ethics* states,

> Social workers should strive to become and remain proficient in professional practice and the performance of professional functions. Social workers should critically examine and keep current with emerging knowledge relevant to social work. Social workers should routinely review the professional literature and participate in continuing education relevant to social work practice and social work ethics. (Standard 4.01[b])

The NAADAC (2021) *Code of Ethics* states:

> Addiction professionals who choose to engage in the use of technology for e-therapy, distance counseling, and e-supervision shall pursue specialized knowledge and competency regarding the technical, ethical, and legal considerations specific to technology, social media, and distance counseling. Providers shall be trained and current in their knowledge of e-therapy technologies and techniques. (Standard VI-2)

Case 3.10: Anne F. and the AI Client Satisfaction Survey

Anne F., a psychiatrist who directs an outpatient clinic for adolescents who struggle with eating disorders, contracted with an AI company that designed a smartphone app and wearable sensors that clinic clients could use to provide clinicians with real-time updates and reports on their symptoms and use of clinical interventions. Anne designed a client satisfaction survey that provided the clinical team with clients' feedback about these AI tools, including what clients found appealing and helpful as well as unappealing and unhelpful, and suggestions to improve these tools.

CONCLUSION

In this chapter, I discussed best practices for the ethical use of AI in behavioral health. I discussed how behavioral health practitioners can draw on core ethics concepts to develop best practices, create ethics-based governing principles, establish a digital ethics steering committee, convene diverse focus groups, subject algorithms to peer review, conduct AI simulations, develop clinician-focused guidance for interpreting AI results, develop rigorous communication and training protocols, maintain a log of AI results to identify positive and negative trends, test algorithms for possible biases and inaccuracies, and continuously monitor algorithmic decision processes. Next, I turn to a discussion of ethics-informed risk management protocols designed to protect AI users (clients and the general public) and behavioral health practitioners.

4

Risk Management and Artificial Intelligence in Behavioral Healthcare

Clearly, AI has the potential to support behavioral health professionals' efforts to assist people who struggle in life. Among other uses, AI can expand users' access to important information about behavioral health, guide users to resources, provide advice and support, enable users to provide practitioners with real-time information about their emotional health and behavior, enable administrators to populate content in documents, and enable practitioners to document their clinical services.

AI also comes with noteworthy risks. Irresponsible or unskilled use of AI can compromise users' privacy, limit their autonomy, misdiagnose users' behavioral health challenges, exacerbate social bias and discrimination, and lead to fraud and plagiarism. Further, negligent and unethical use of AI can expose practitioners to the risk of being named in lawsuits and licensing board complaints. In this respect, it is important for behavioral health practitioners to engage in sound risk management protocols to protect clients, the general public, and themselves.

CONCEPT OF RISK MANAGEMENT: A BRIEF OVERVIEW

Risk management is a broad term that refers to efforts to protect clients, practitioners, supervisors, and employers. Risk management includes the prevention of lawsuits and licensing board complaints alleging, for example, the negligent or unethical use of AI. Risk management also includes prevention of ethics complaints filed with national professional associations, such as the NASW, ACA, and AAMFT (Barsky, 2024; Reamer, 2023d). Lawsuits allege professional malpractice. Licensing board complaints generally allege violation of standards of practice set forth in licensing statutes and regulations. Ethics complaints filed with professional associations allege violation of their respective codes of conduct.

Lawsuits can result in settlements or monetary judgments against practitioners. Licensing board complaints can result in fines, public notice of findings, revocation or suspension of a professional license, probation, mandated evaluation or supervision (clinical or ethical) and continuing education, reprimand, or censure. Complaints filed against members of professional associations can result in various types of corrective action or sanctions. *Corrective action* can include options, such as training (for example, in the proper use of AI consistent with prevailing ethical standards), supervision, consultation censure, restitution, or compensation. *Sanctions* can include, among other options, a reprimand, public notice of findings, membership suspension, membership termination, and notification of licensing boards and malpractice insurers.

In the United States, malpractice payments and healthcare-related adverse actions associated with the improper use of AI are reportable to the federal National Practitioner Data Bank (NPDB), maintained by the DHHS. The *NPDB* is a web-based repository of reports containing information on malpractice payments and certain adverse actions related to healthcare practitioners, providers, and suppliers. Established by Congress in 1986, the NPDB is a tool that prevents practitioners from moving from state to state without disclosure or discovery of previous damaging conduct or performance. It can be accessed by authorized users, such as hospitals, state licensing boards, and professional societies with formal peer review. Settlements and verdicts are reportable to state licensing boards (Reamer, 2023d).

Professional malpractice is generally considered a form of negligence. The concept applies to professionals who are required to perform in a manner consistent with the legal concept of the *substantive standard of care* in the profession, which is generally defined as the way a reasonable and prudent professional should have acted under the same or similar circumstances, for example, related to behavioral health practitioners' use of AI. Malpractice in behavioral health usually is the result of a practitioner's active violation of a client's rights (in legal terms, acts of commission, misfeasance, or malfeasance) or a practitioner's failure to perform certain duties (acts of omission, also known as nonfeasance).

Some malpractice claims result from genuine mistakes, for example, inadvertent breaches of confidentiality by practitioners who use AI or failure to disclose to users possible risks associated with AI. Other claims arise from a deliberate decision to risk a claim (for example, a practitioner decides to use AI to provide after-hours support to high-risk clients). A practitioner's unethical behavior or misconduct (for example, using an inexpensive AI tool that the practitioner knew was developed by a company with no expertise in behavioral health) can also trigger claims.

In general, malpractice occurs when evidence exists that four conditions have been met. First, at the time of the alleged malpractice, the practitioner owed a legal duty to the client (for example, users of AI tools made available by the practitioner). Second, the practitioner was derelict in that duty either through *omission*, the failure to perform a duty (such as failing to notify clients about possible limitations associated with their use of AI tools provided by the practitioner), or *commission* (for example, using an AI tool that was not developed responsibly by professionals who have behavioral health knowledge and expertise). Third, the client suffered some harm or injury (for example, the client alleges that they suffered emotional distress and required additional psychiatric care after they had relied on an AI tool made available by a practitioner that did not meet widely held standards and that misdiagnosed the client's mental health challenges). Fourth, the professional's dereliction of duty was the direct and proximate cause of the harm or injury (for example, the client's injuries were the result of the practitioner's irresponsible or unethical use of the AI tool).

Licensing boards use different criteria when adjudicating complaints alleging improper use of AI. In contrast to courts of law that adjudicate lawsuits, licensing boards need not require evidence that practitioners' actions (commission) or inactions (omission) caused harm. Rather, practitioners can be sanctioned based simply on evidence that their conduct violated standards contained in licensing statutes and regulations pertaining to the use of AI without any evidence of harm. Professional associations that process ethics complaints filed against members can be sanctioned based simply on evidence that the practitioner's conduct violated standards in the association's code of conduct or code of ethics.

Lawsuits filed against behavioral health practitioners fall into two broad groups. The first includes claims that allege that practitioners carried out their duties—for example, the manner in which they used AI—improperly or in a fashion inconsistent with the profession's standard of care (either by commission or misfeasance/malfeasance). The distinction between misfeasance and malfeasance is an important one with respect to behavioral health practitioners' use of AI. *Misfeasance* is ordinarily defined as the commission of a proper act in a wrongful or injurious manner or the improper performance of an act that might have been performed lawfully. Examples include flawed informed consent procedures when using AI or use of AI technology that inadvertently breached a user's private information. *Malfeasance* is ordinarily defined as the commission of a wrongful or unlawful act. Examples include the deliberate use of what a practitioner knows is a flawed AI tool that often misdiagnoses clients' symptoms.

The second broad category includes claims that allege that practitioners failed to carry out a duty that they are ordinarily expected to carry out in accordance with their profession's standard of care (acts of omission, also known as nonfeasance). Examples include behavioral health practitioners who fail to create and implement sound informed consent and confidentiality protocols when using AI.

Malpractice suits have their origin in early English common law (Reamer, 2023d). Lawsuits that allege malpractice are *civil suits* (in contrast to criminal proceedings). Ordinarily civil suits are based on tort or contract law and involve *plaintiffs*—the individuals bringing the suit—seeking some form of redress for injuries that they claim to have incurred. These injuries may be economic (for example, lost wages or the cost involved in seeking psychiatric care because of a flawed AI tool that led to a clinical misdiagnosis), physical (for example, resulting from a suicide attempt as a result of a client's misdiagnosis by a flawed AI tool), or emotional (for example, depression or anxiety brought about by a flawed AI tool's misdiagnosis of symptoms).

As in criminal trials, defendants in civil suits are presumed blameless until proved otherwise. In ordinary civil suits, the standard of proof required to find defendants liable for their actions is *preponderance of the evidence*, meaning that plaintiffs must prove that it is more likely or probable than not that defendants are liable because of the negligent ways in which they used AI. This is in contrast to the stricter standard of proof beyond a reasonable doubt used in criminal proceedings.

Most legal actions against behavioral health practitioners involve *tort law*, that is, law involving private or civil wrongs or injuries resulting from a breach of a legal duty. Torts may be unintentional (negligent) or intentional. *Unintentional torts* concern allegations that the practitioner's performance—for example, related to their inadvertent use of flawed consent-to-treat protocols when offering clients AI tools—fell below the standard of care for the profession. *Intentional torts* do not require evidence of negligence. Most tort claims against behavioral health practitioners allege some form of malpractice (unintentional torts).

Case 4.1: Danielle M. and the Malpractice Suit

Danielle M., a psychiatrist, is medical director of an outpatient psychiatric clinic that specializes in the treatment of mood disorders. Danielle oversaw implementation of a smartphone app patients can use to share their symptoms with clinic staffers, access self-help resources, request appointments, and send messages to clinic staffers. The app uses AI to respond to patient's queries about management of their symptoms.

One patient, who struggled with major depressive disorder, used the app amid an emotional crisis that included panic attack symptoms and suicidal ideation. The app posed a series of questions to the patient and generated suggestions about ways to engage in self-care, such as breathing and mindfulness exercises. The patient followed the advice but continued to experience panic symptoms and suicidal thoughts. That evening, the patient attempted suicide by overdosing on prescribed neuroleptic medication. The patient survived the suicide attempt and, after receiving inpatient treatment, sued the clinic and Danielle, alleging malpractice. The lawsuit alleged that the clinic and Danielle failed to provide sufficient disclaimers about the limitations of the app during a mental health crisis or with sufficient advice about what a patient should do in the event of an emergency. The patient also filed a licensing board complaint against Danielle.

STANDARDS OF CARE AND AI

The first required condition of a malpractice claim—evidence that the practitioner owed a legal duty to the injured party—is often the easiest to satisfy. Clearly, a behavioral health practitioner who uses AI to serve clients owes a duty of care to these clients.

Determining whether the practitioner was somehow derelict in the performance of that duty, the second condition, typically is much more complex. Here, questions ordinarily arise that relate to the prevailing standard of care in the relevant behavioral health profession. Although many standards of care are similar across the various behavioral health professions, some noteworthy differences are linked to the respective professions' unique ethical standards, treatment protocols, and licensing statutes and regulations. Although jurisdictions have varying descriptions of the standard of care, the common principle requires the practitioner do what a reasonable person of ordinary prudence would do in the practitioner's place, for example, related to the practitioner's use of AI (Reamer, 2023d).

For many years, courts defined "standard of care" by comparing a practitioner's actions with those of similarly trained professionals in the same community—what is generally known as the *locality rule*. The assumption here was that levels of expertise and training varied from community to community as a function of local training programs and access to technology and treatment techniques. One practical consequence of the locality rule was that expert witnesses in a malpractice case usually came from the local community. This practice preceded the invention of AI and its use by behavioral health professionals.

Over time, many jurisdictions have overturned the locality rule either by judicial decision or legislation. The rationale has been that changes in modern communication (especially the advent of the internet and the proliferation of digital technology), transportation, and education have provided practitioners with much greater access to updated information about developments in their profession. This is especially true regarding AI, which is now a common phenomenon across all jurisdictions in which behavioral healthcare is practiced. Consequently, courts now typically permit out-of-state expert witnesses to testify in malpractice cases. That is, the standard of care involving the use of technology, such as AI, tends to be based on national, rather than local, norms in a profession.

Some departures from the standard of care are relatively easy to prove. A behavioral health practitioner who discloses on their personal Facebook site clients' confidential information generated by AI would clearly violate the standard of care as would a practitioner who deliberately falsifies AI-generated clinical notes that they edit.

Far more common, however, are those cases in which reasonable and prudent practitioners may disagree about the appropriateness of a practitioner's actions, that is, whether those actions constituted a departure from the standard of care. This is especially true with respect to behavioral health practitioners' use of AI given that this is a relatively new phenomenon in the history of behavioral healthcare for which ethical standards are emerging. It is not hard to imagine that expert witnesses drawn from behavioral health professions might disagree with one another about the nature and application of ethical standards relevant to AI.

In litigation cases, lawyers typically retain experts for consultation about whether the practitioner's conduct met or breached the standard of care. Currently, the number of behavioral health practitioners who are truly expert regarding the use of AI is relatively limited.

In theory, the issue before the jury in a malpractice case involving questions about a practitioner's use of AI is not to determine whether the defendant practitioner used the *best* approach but, rather, whether the defendant used a *reasonable* approach that met the standard of care. The standard of care essentially describes a minimally acceptable level of professional competence pertaining to the use of AI. In practice, however, the jury will be forced to decide what the standard of care requires with respect to a practitioner's use of AI. The jury assesses the credibility and experience of the expert witnesses and the parties.

The reality is that in the relatively new world of AI in behavioral healthcare, reasonable minds may differ with regard to the appropriateness of a defendant practitioner's use of AI. What matters especially is whether a behavioral health practitioner's conclusion about the use of AI in particular circumstances was a reasonable decision in light of the relevant information available *at that time*, recognizing that some colleagues may have reached a different conclusion. Behavioral health practitioners should recognize that if they present themselves to the public as specialists regarding their use of AI, they may be judged by the standard of care applicable to a specialist with this expertise even if the practitioner's claim of expertise is a misrepresentation.

Demonstrating the third condition of a malpractice claim—that the client who used AI made available by the practitioner suffered some harm or injury—can also be difficult in behavioral health. In behavioral healthcare, alleged harms are often difficult to document empirically, especially if they are allegedly associated with practitioners' negligent use of AI. In many instances, plaintiffs claim that they have experienced some form of emotional injury or harm as opposed to some form of physical injury. In these cases, the plaintiff may have some difficulty substantiating the injury, especially if the plaintiff has a so-called preexisting condition, that is, the plaintiff had been treated for similar symptoms or diagnoses before the alleged malpractice (for example, clinical depression, anxiety). Compelling expert testimony about the negligent use of AI may be required to present a strong case that the alleged malpractice caused harm independent of any prior conditions.

This suggests that a plaintiff can find it difficult to satisfy the fourth condition of a malpractice claim—that the practitioner's dereliction of duty (for example, related to the practitioner's allegedly negligent use of AI) was the direct and proximate cause of the harm or injury. Some jurisdictions describe the proximate cause requirement by using a so-called "but for" analysis, that is, but for the alleged misconduct related to a practitioner's use of AI, the harm would not have occurred. Other jurisdictions may use a "substantial contributing cause" standard for proving proximate cause. Under any approach, however, this element likely will be vigorously contested with respect to practitioners' alleged AI-related negligence (Reamer, 2023d).

Even plaintiffs who can document that they sustained some sort of injury—for example, emotional distress, depression, or physical harm—may have difficulty demonstrating that the practitioner's alleged dereliction of duty associated with the use of AI was the *direct* and *proximate* cause of the injury. For instance, strong evidence may exist that a client manifested symptoms of depression after a practitioner's chatbot misdiagnosed a client's symptoms. The practitioner's defense attorney might argue, however, that this client had a long-standing history of depression that preceded the clinician's treatment of the client and that a variety of other stressful events in the client's life at the time of the inadvertent AI-related misdiagnosis may account for the depression.

Some malpractice cases in behavioral health are relatively clear-cut. A practitioner in a residential setting who did not ensure that an AI-generated clinical note included evidence of a client's suicidal ideation may clearly be liable if staffers on the next shift, who reviewed the most recent AI-generated notes and were unaware of the suicide risk, consequently failed to monitor the resident closely, and the client was injured seriously in an actual suicide attempt. Similarly, a practitioner in private practice who neglected to discuss informed consent with a client who shared sensitive information on an AI tool used by the private practice, failed to have the client sign a consent form, and then disclosed diagnostic information shared by the client to the client's employer clearly may be liable if that employer then fires the client based on the information shared by the practitioner. In those instances, malpractice and negligence may be relatively easy to establish.

There is likely to be less consensus in instances in which behavioral health practitioners use AI. In many liability cases, a judge or jury can find it quite difficult to determine what, exactly, constitutes the standard of care in the profession regarding a practitioner's actual decisions and actions related to the use of AI. The same holds for licensing board cases: Board members may have difficulty reaching consensus about practitioners' use of AI. Attorneys and expert witnesses often present strong arguments in conflicting directions.

In such circumstances in which lawyers and expert witnesses cannot offer unequivocal and indisputable evidence regarding the extent to which a practitioner's conduct related to the use of AI met the standard of care, the legal debate about the standard of care may shift from the practitioner's actual decision and actions related to the substantive issue at hand regarding the use of AI or the outcome of the decision and toward the process and procedures that the practitioner followed to make the decision about the use of AI. That is, the line of questioning may focus instead on the steps that the practitioner took (or should have taken but did not take) to make a sound decision about whether and how to use AI.

Case 4.2: Carla F. and Standard of Care

Carla F. is a mental health counselor in private practice. After being in practice for more than two decades, Carla grew weary of the amount of uncompensated time she spent documenting her clinical sessions. Based on a colleague's advice, Carla began subscribing to an AI documentation product that generated Carla's clinical notes from recordings of clinical sessions that Carla uploaded to the company's platform.

One of Carla's clients, who had been diagnosed with bipolar disorder, was in the midst of a contentious child custody dispute. The client had stopped taking their bipolar medication because of their concern about side effects. One evening, when dropping their children off at the mother's apartment following a scheduled visit, the client got into a bitter argument with the mother. The client, who carried a weapon, shot and killed the mother. Later, the client was arrested, charged with murder, and was convicted.

The victim's estate sued Carla, alleging that she was negligent in her treatment of the client's bipolar symptoms and failed to meet the standard of care. The plaintiff's lawyer subpoenaed Carla's clinical records and learned that all of the session notes had been generated by AI software. The lawyer reviewed the notes carefully and identified several key errors regarding diagnoses and services provided. While Carla was on the witness stand and under oath, the lawyer projected the AI-generated notes on an LED screen and questioned Carla about how the notes were created and about the errors. In her testimony, Carla admitted that she used the AI documentation software to save time and had not carefully proofread the notes that contained errors. The attorney used this evidence to impeach Carla's credibility and question her ability to meet the standards of care in mental health counseling.

PROCEDURAL STANDARD OF CARE

The *procedural standard of care*—the steps a reasonable and prudent practitioner should take to make a sound decision in complex circumstances that may lead reasonable practitioners to reach different conclusions—includes nine key elements that are especially relevant to practitioners' potential or actual use of AI (Reamer, 2023d):

1. **Review relevant ethical standards:** Practitioners who consider using AI must consult relevant codes of ethics applicable to their respective professions that have standards related to the use of AI (for example, related to informed consent, client privacy, client confidentiality, nondiscrimination). Contemporary codes of ethics provide extensive guidelines concerning the ethical use of digital and other technology; these guidelines are often referenced during litigation proceedings. Also, many licensing boards have adopted these codes of ethics, or portions of them, in their regulations.

2. **Consult colleagues:** Practitioners who consider using AI should consult colleagues who have specialized knowledge or expertise related to the use of AI in behavioral healthcare, including ethics experts. Practitioners in private or independent practice should participate in peer consultation groups. Practitioners employed in settings that

have ethics committees (that is, committees that provide staff with a forum for consultation on difficult cases) should take advantage of this form of consultation when they consider using AI. Also, practitioners may be able to obtain consultation advice about the use of AI from their malpractice insurer or professional association. Practitioners who are sued or who have licensing board complaints filed against them associated with their use of AI can help demonstrate their competent decision-making skills by showing that they sought consultation.

3. Obtain appropriate supervision: Behavioral health practitioners who have access to a supervisor should consult the supervisor about the possible use of AI. Supervisors may be able to help practitioners navigate complicated challenges or refer practitioners to knowledgeable AI experts. Practitioners who are sued can help demonstrate their competent decision-making skills by showing that they sought supervision pertaining to their use of AI.

4. Review relevant regulations, laws, and policies: Practitioners who use or consider using AI should always consider relevant federal, state, and local regulations and laws (prominent examples of federal laws in the United States include the HIPAA of 1996 and the 2017 Title 42 CFR Part 2).

5. Review relevant practice standards: National professional associations—such as the ACA, National Board for Certified Counselors, NASW, APA, American Psychiatric Association, AAMFT, and NAADAC—periodically adopt formal practice standards developed by task forces. Examples include national standards pertaining to the use of technology to serve clients, including, for instance, a tip sheet developed by NASW (n.d.). These prominent standards may be introduced as evidence in litigation and licensing board cases associated with practitioners' use of AI.

6. Review employers' policies: Many behavioral health organizations have developed and promulgated formal policies governing employees' use of digital and other forms of technology, including AI. These policies may provide useful guidance. In addition, these policies may be introduced as evidence in litigation and licensing board cases associated with practitioners' use of AI.

7. Review relevant literature: Practitioners who use or are considering using AI should consult literature related to the use of AI in behavioral healthcare. Consulting this literature can provide useful guidance and helpful evidence that a practitioner made a conscientious attempt to comply with current standards in the field related to the use of AI. In addition, practitioners can expect that opposing lawyers will conduct their own comprehensive review of relevant literature related to the use of AI in behavioral healthcare to locate authoritative publications that support their legal theory and clients' claims. Lawyers often submit as evidence copies of publications that, in their opinion, buttress their legal case. Lawyers may use the authors of influential publications as expert witnesses.

8. Obtain legal consultation when necessary: Practitioners who use or are considering using AI should recognize that there may be relevant statutes, regulations, and court decisions that they need to consider. Consulting a knowledgeable healthcare law attorney can provide useful guidance when practitioners develop AI-related policies and protocols. Further, the fact that a practitioner took the time to obtain legal consultation about the proper use of AI provides additional evidence of having made conscientious, diligent efforts to handle the situation professionally and ethically.

9. Document decision-making steps: Thorough documentation of the steps that practitioners took regarding their use of AI is essential, especially if they are named in lawsuits and ethics complaints associated with their use of AI. Creating a comprehensive, detailed paper or digital trail demonstrating the conscientious steps the practitioner took when making decisions about the use of AI can provide powerful evidence when practitioners need to defend themselves during the legal proceedings.

The extent to which a behavioral health practitioner engaged in these steps when making a decision about the use of AI may become a key issue during a lawsuit. For example, during a *deposition*—a method of pretrial discovery that consists of a witness's statement and responses to questioning under oath—or actual trial, an opposing attorney in the case might ask which supervisors the practitioner consulted about the use of AI. Were these supervisors the most appropriate ones to consult given their areas of expertise? Did the practitioner mention the AI-related issue in peer consultation? Did the practitioner consult a lawyer about the legal implications of the use of AI? Did the practitioner consult the relevant code of ethics, practice standards, organizational policies, and literature related to the use of AI? Did the practitioner document these various steps?

The standard of care related to the use of AI in behavioral health can be viewed in two ways. First, the standard of care may focus on a practitioner's specific decisions or actions pertaining to their use of AI. Second, the standard of care may focus on the process and procedures that the practitioner followed in making the relevant decision or pursuing a course of action related to the use of AI (that is, the practitioner's use of supervision, collegial and legal consultation, literature review, review of code of ethics standards, organizational policies, and practice standards).

Case 4.3: Gary R. and the Risk Management Plan

Gary R. is a social worker at a mental health center that was considering adding a chatbot to its website that would allow members of the general public, current clients, and prospective clients to seek information about mental health symptoms and challenges, schedule appointments, and obtain self-help and other resources. Gary recognized that he and his mental health center colleagues needed to identify relevant ethical and risk management issues to comply with prevailing ethical standards in behavioral healthcare and relevant laws. Gary created a detailed plan that included several steps preceding any rollout of the chatbot, including brainstorming with colleagues about ethical and risk management issues; consulting with a behavioral health ethics expert and an attorney who specializes in behavioral health risk management; reviewing literature on ethical issues associated with the use of AI; reviewing relevant code of ethics and technology-related practice standards; and conferring with the mental health center's malpractice insurer about applicable coverage.

PRIVACY AUDITS

Increasing numbers of behavioral health agencies and practitioners are conducting what are known as *privacy audits* to ensure compliance with current national standards (Reamer, 2023d). Privacy audits are especially relevant in settings that use AI.

In the United States, many of the current privacy audit standards were developed with two prominent sets of federal standards in mind: (1) the HIPAA of 1996 and (2) the 2009 HITECH Act. Any healthcare provider that deals with PHI, which may include AI data, must ensure that all the required physical and network security measures are in place and followed (Reamer, 2023d).

The 2009 HITECH Act, part of the American Recovery and Reinvestment Act of 2009, includes provisions requiring organizations to conduct privacy audits. Subtitle D of the HITECH Act addresses the privacy and security concerns associated with the electronic transmission of health information, in part, through several provisions that strengthen the civil and criminal enforcement of the 1996 HIPAA rules. Healthcare organizations and third-party payers are expected to monitor for breaches of PHI from both internal and external sources.

The U.S. Office for Civil Rights (OCR) has established criteria that its auditors use to validate compliance with federal regulations. OCR provides a useful guide for behavioral health agencies and practitioners who use AI. Key audit activities include the following:

Determine the activities that will be tracked or audited. Obtain and review documentation to determine whether audit controls have been implemented over information systems that contain or use PHI.

Select the tools that will be deployed for auditing and system activity reviews. Inquire of management as to whether systems and applications have been evaluated to determine whether upgrades are necessary. Obtain and review documentation of tools or applications that management has identified to capture the appropriate audit information.

Develop and deploy the information review/audit policy. Obtain and review formal or informal policies and procedures and evaluate the content to understand whether a formal audit policy is in place to communicate the details of the entity's audits and reviews to the workforce. Obtain and review an email, or some form of communication, showing that the audit policy is communicated to the workforce.

Develop appropriate standard operating procedures. Obtain and review management's procedures in place to determine the systems and applications to be audited and how they will be audited.

The American Health Information Management Association (AHIMA)—a prominent organization dedicated to improving the management of health-related information—has developed comprehensive protocols for professionals who want to conduct privacy audits. Their guidelines are especially valuable for behavioral health practitioners and agencies that use AI.

According to AHIMA (Adler, 2017), privacy audits should produce detailed audit logs that are useful for the following:

- Detecting unauthorized access to client information
- Establishing a culture of responsibility and accountability
- Reducing the risk associated with inappropriate access
- Providing forensic evidence during investigations of suspected and known security incidents and breaches to client privacy, especially if sanctions against a workforce member, business associate, or other contracted agent will be applied
- Tracking disclosures of PHI
- Responding to client privacy concerns regarding unauthorized access by family members, friends, or others
- Evaluating the overall effectiveness of the organization's policy and user education regarding appropriate access and use of client information (this includes comparing actual workforce activity to expected activity and discovering where additional training or education may be necessary to reduce errors)
- Detecting new threats and intrusion attempts
- Identifying potential problems
- Addressing compliance with regulatory and accreditation requirements

Several behavioral health professionals and their employers have discovered significant security breaches that led to online exposure of clients' sensitive health and behavioral health information (Reamer, 2023d). Investigations of such breaches conducted by the federal OCR can result in significant civil monetary penalties and publicly available disclosure on the agency's website (Reamer, 2023d). These incidents provide a cautionary tale for behavioral health practitioners who use AI.

Case 4.4: Anne Marie D. and the Privacy Audit

Anne Marie D. is the director of social work at an outpatient psychiatric clinic. Her hospital uses AI in several ways, including providing the general public with behavioral health information and resources with its chatbot, providing current clients with access to a smartphone app that allows them to transmit information about their symptoms and goal achievement to clinic staffers, providing current clients with wearable sensors that transmit key health information to clinic staffers, and providing clinicians with access to an AI tool they can use to generate clinical notes.

Anne Marie was concerned about the large volumes of PHI that are transmitted to clinic staffers using AI and stored on the clinic's and third-party companies' platforms. She met with the clinic's chief executive officer to share her concerns. The two then met with the attorney who oversees the clinic's risk management protocols. At the conclusion of this meeting, the three agreed that the clinic needed to conduct a formal privacy audit to ensure that proper security measures are in place and to comply with national standards.

MALPRACTICE INSURANCE

Behavioral health practitioners who use AI can obtain comprehensive liability insurance that offers legal defense coverage and indemnifies practitioners against liability (Reamer, 2023d). Policies are available that cover individual practitioners, behavioral health agencies, corporations, students, and educational programs. These liability policies typically contain options with regard to the amount of coverage (for example, the amount of coverage for each wrongful act, or series of related wrongful acts, and the amount of aggregate coverage during a given policy period, such as a year), coverage during extended reporting periods (that is, coverage for claims filed against a practitioner after the end of the policy period), and coverage of employees (as in a private group practice).

A typical policy is known as a *claims-made policy*, which means that the coverage is limited to liability for only those claims that are first made against the policyholder and reported to the company during the period the policy is in force. Practitioners who also want to be insured for claims associated with their use of AI made after terminating the policy need to pay an additional premium for extended reporting period protection; this is known as *tail coverage*.

Some insurers also offer what is known as nose coverage (also known as prior acts coverage). A basic claims-made policy will only cover claims associated with services that were provided while the policy is in effect. *Nose coverage* is a supplement to an expiring claims-made malpractice insurance policy that may be purchased from a new carrier when a practitioner changes carriers and had claims-made coverage with a previous carrier. Nose coverage will provide protection under the new policy if claims are reported in the future for treatment dates going back to the previous policy's inception date.

Behavioral health practitioners who use AI also have the option to purchase so-called *occurrence malpractice coverage*. An occurrence policy has lifetime coverage for the incidents that occur during a policy period, regardless of when the claim is reported. A claims-made policy typically is less expensive initially than an occurrence policy; the premium matures over a number of years (for example, five years).

With dramatic increases in behavioral health practitioners' use of digital and other technology, such as AI, to provide services to clients remotely, communicate with clients, and store sensitive information electronically, it is important to have what is known as *cyber-liability coverage*. This policy provides coverage in the event of a data breach on a practitioner's computer, smartphone, or electronic client records. A *data breach*, or security incident, occurs when confidential client data, such as electronic records or personal financial data, are taken, copied, transmitted, viewed, stolen, or used by any individual unauthorized to handle the information. Even if practitioners who use AI retain a third-party company, such as a data storage provider, they can be held responsible for data breaches caused by them. Such a policy may provide coverage for legal expenses, breach notification expenses, and damages and fines in the event of a data breach.

Even behavioral health practitioners employed in settings that provide group liability coverage to employees should seriously consider obtaining their own individual coverage and maximizing the amount of coverage, especially for licensing board defense that may be associated with AI use (Reamer, 2023d). When a liability claim names both the practitioner and the worker's employer, the employer could argue that the practitioner, and not the employing agency, was negligent in the way they used AI. This can create a conflict of interest. Individual coverage would thus protect workers who find themselves at odds with their employers in relation to a liability claim, particularly if the employer is unwilling to retain separate legal counsel for the practitioner.

Also, individual policies typically include a provision that will cover legal expenses if a practitioner retains an attorney to assist in responding to a complaint filed with a state licensing board. An employer's policy may not provide coverage for this legal representation.

Further, *individual coverage* protects individual practitioners if claims against their employer's insurance policy exceed that policy's limits (for example, if a case involving client suicide that was linked with AI use leads to a $5.75 million judgment against an employer's insurance policy that has a $3 million limit). Individual coverage offers protection to practitioners who leave their employment setting before a lawsuit is filed that alleges the practitioner was negligent during the time of employment with respect to their use of AI.

NOTE: Practitioners also should remember to immediately notify their insurance companies in the event of a potential or actual claim or lawsuit associated with AI use. Failure to do so can void coverage under the policy.

Although liability claims and lawsuits filed against practitioners are relatively rare, professionals must have a keen understanding of legal concepts related to malpractice, negligence, and liability as they pertain to AI use. Statistically, licensing board complaints filed against practitioners are more common, although most practitioners will complete their careers without being named in one (Reamer, 2023d). Fortunately, behavioral health practitioners can take a number of steps to help prevent lawsuits and licensing board complaints.

Case 4.5: Juan D. and Malpractice Insurance

Juan D. is a psychologist who works in the outpatient eating disorders clinic at a large metropolitan hospital. One of Juan's clients has struggled with anorexia and depression. As part of the program, Juan's client used a wearable sensor that transmitted AI-generated health and behavioral health information to the clinic. Juan's client also used a clinic-sponsored app to communicate with Juan.

Juan's client attempted to die by suicide by swallowing a large amount of her psychotropic medication. She was hospitalized for three weeks and then transferred to an out-of-state residential treatment program. The client filed a licensing board complaint against Juan that alleged he had not been sufficiently responsive to her repeated requests for emotional support and other forms of assistance. The client claimed that Juan abandoned her and that this triggered her suicide attempt.

Juan received the notice of the licensing board complaint, which requested all of his clinical records, including all relevant ESI (for example, text messages exchanged through the client's smartphone app, online social networking posts, all content generated by AI tools). On the advice of a colleague, Juan retained an attorney who specializes in defending behavioral health practitioners who are named in licensing board complaints. Juan informed the clinic director about the licensing board complaint and requested that the hospital cover his legal expenses. A hospital vice president informed Juan that the hospital's malpractice coverage applies only to lawsuits, not licensing board complaints. The vice president explained to Juan that since the complaint was filed against his license, and not against the hospital, Juan would be personally responsible for the legal fees.

EVOLUTION OF ETHICS-INFORMED STANDARDS

Ethics-informed standards pertaining to behavioral health practitioners' use of AI are evolving. It is essential that practitioners know about national and international efforts to develop and refine these standards.

There have been several significant efforts to develop such standards. For example, in 2023, President Joseph R. Biden, Jr., issued an executive order requiring development of risk management policies and protocols associated with AI (The White House, 2023). Specifically, the executive order mandated creation of unprecedented standards that are particularly relevant to behavioral health organizations and practitioners that use or are considering using AI. The standards

- require that developers of AI systems share their safety test results and other critical information with the U.S. government.
- develop standards, tools, and tests to help ensure that AI systems are safe, secure, and trustworthy.

- protect citizens from AI-enabled fraud and deception by establishing standards and best practices for detecting AI-generated content and authenticating official content.
- establish an advanced cybersecurity program to develop AI tools to find and fix vulnerabilities in critical software.
- protect citizens' privacy by prioritizing federal support for accelerating the development and use of privacy-preserving techniques—including ones that use cutting-edge AI and that let AI systems be trained while preserving the privacy of the training data.
- strengthen privacy-preserving research and technologies, such as cryptographic tools that preserve individuals' privacy.
- evaluate how agencies collect and use commercially available information—including information they procure from data brokers—and strengthen privacy guidance for federal agencies to account for AI risks.
- develop guidelines for federal agencies to evaluate the effectiveness of privacy-preserving techniques, including those used in AI systems.
- provide clear guidance to landlords, federal benefits programs, and federal contractors to keep AI algorithms from being used to exacerbate discrimination.
- address algorithmic discrimination through training, technical assistance, and coordination between the Department of Justice and federal civil rights offices on best practices for investigating and prosecuting civil rights violations related to AI.
- ensure fairness throughout the criminal justice system by developing best practices on the use of AI in sentencing, parole and probation, pretrial release and detention, risk assessments, surveillance, crime forecasting and predictive policing, and forensic analysis.
- advance the responsible use of AI in healthcare, development of affordable and lifesaving drugs, and prevent unsafe healthcare practices involving AI.
- shape AI's potential to transform education by creating resources to support educators deploying AI-enabled educational tools, such as personalized tutoring in schools.

- develop principles and best practices to mitigate the harms and maximize the benefits of AI for workers by addressing job displacement; labor standards; workplace equity, health, and safety; and data collection; these principles and best practices will benefit workers by providing guidance to prevent employers from undercompensating workers, evaluating job applications unfairly, or impinging on workers' ability to organize.
- accelerate development and implementation of AI standards with international partners and in standards organizations, ensuring that the technology is safe, secure, trustworthy, and interoperable.
- promote the safe, responsible, and rights-affirming development and deployment of AI abroad to solve global challenges, such as advancing sustainable development and mitigating dangers to critical infrastructure.

In 2024, the National Institute of Standards and Technology (NIST, 2024) promulgated a comprehensive risk management framework pertaining to AI. This framework is the result of input from the NIST Generative AI Public Working Group that includes more than 2,500 members. The AI guidance document presents a list of 13 risks and more than 400 actions that developers can take to manage them. The risks include issues such as easier access to information related to chemical, biological, radiological, or nuclear weapons; a lowered barrier to entry for hacking, malware, phishing, and other cybersecurity attacks; and the production of hate speech and toxic, denigrating or stereotyping content.

In 2021, the member states of the United Nations Educational, Scientific and Cultural Organization (UNESCO) adopted formal recommendations on the ethical use of AI. This pioneering document addresses innovative tools, methodologies, and initiatives to maximize the positive effects of AI while addressing the associated risks. These recommendations have provided guidance throughout the world for development of ethics-informed policies governing the use of AI (Sarraf, 2021; UNESCO, 2021).

UNESCO's Global AI Ethics and Governance Observatory issued recommendations that focus on who should be in control of AI technology and encourage governments around the world to establish institutional and legal frameworks to govern the use of AI and ensure that this technology contributes to the public good (UNESCO, 2023). The Observatory highlighted a set of ethics-based values related to human rights, human dignity, and environmental sustainability. Specific recommendations concern the effects of AI on decision making; employment and labor; social interaction; healthcare; education; media; access to information; digital divide; personal data and consumer protection; environment; democracy; rule of law; security and policing; and human rights and fundamental freedoms, including freedom of expression, privacy, and nondiscrimination.

The Observatory also recommended implementation of "ethical impact statements" related to the use of AI (UNESCO, 2023). The principal purpose of an *ethical impact statement* is to identify and assess benefits, concerns, and risks of AI systems as well as appropriate risk prevention, mitigation, and monitoring measures. Such assessments, which are directly relevant to behavioral health practitioners, identify potential effects of AI on human rights and fundamental freedoms, in particular, the rights of marginalized and vulnerable people or people in vulnerable situations, labor rights, and the environment and ecosystems (including the effect of AI on carbon footprint, energy consumption, and the environmental effects of raw material extraction for supporting the manufacturing of AI technologies). Specifically, ethical impact statements address the following topics and questions:

A description of the AI project: What is the nature of the AI project and its key aims?

Proportionality screening and "do no harm": Has careful consideration been given to non-AI options that may be used to achieve the same goal? If so, why is the option involving an AI system favored? Has the scope of this project been clearly defined? What limitations have been placed on the scope of this project to ensure it remains proportional to the stated objective? Are the expected effects irreversible or difficult to reverse, or could they involve life-and-death decisions (for example, setting prison sentences or determining medical treatments)? Could the AI system and its application impact fundamental human rights (for example, human dignity, freedom of expression, fair trial)?

Project governance: Who has ultimate decision-making authority within the project team responsible for this AI system? Has consideration been given to the diversity of the AI project team, especially in terms of, but not limited to, gender, age, race, color, descent, language, religion, national origin, ethnic origin, social origin, economic or social condition, disability, and sexual orientation? To what extent does this representation reflect the complexity and diversity of expected user populations? Is there a potential for bias?

Multistakeholder governance: What stakeholder groups are most likely to be impacted by the deployment of the AI system? Who has the greatest needs for this tool? Who has the least power to influence the development of this tool? Which stakeholder groups will be consulted during the development, deployment, and use of the AI system? How will stakeholders be engaged?

Safety and security: What measures were put in place to ensure the safety and security of the AI system and protect it from system manipulation? How will the sponsor know if the training data or data being processed by the AI system were poisoned or corrupted, or if the system is manipulated?

Fairness, nondiscrimination, and diversity: Has the algorithm been tested with different demographic groups? Was there a difference in terms of accuracy rate (or any other performance metric used)? Was there a discriminatory effect for particular groups? Has there been an analysis of the data to prevent societal and historical biases in data? Are the data well balanced, and do they reflect the diversity of the targeted end-user population? Does the design allow all people, especially marginalized groups (including people with disabilities and people who are economically vulnerable) to access and interact with the AI system? To which segment of the population will the AI system be applied? Is the population affected particularly marginalized?

Sustainability: Has the sponsor consulted relevant environmental policies and laws and estimated the environmental effects of raw material extraction, processing, and transportation involved in manufacturing the hardware of the AI system?

Privacy and data protection: What types of personal data does the AI system have access to? If the data are coming from external entities, are there written agreements detailing the conditions for data sharing? Are the data being stored at a level of security commensurate with their sensitivity? Are the data anonymized or pseudonymized? Do people actively consent for the processing of their data by the AI system? Can users request the deletion of their data and stop the processing by the AI system? If the data are accessible to third parties, are there provisions to protect against ill-intentioned actions?

Human oversight and determination: If the AI system took over a task that was previously conducted by humans, how was the knowledge transfer preserved? How involved in the development and training of the AI system were the humans who previously had conducted the task? If the AI system has the authority to make a decision that would impact people, is the decision subjected to meaningful human oversight before it takes effect? Is it always possible to attribute ethical and legal responsibility for any stage of the lifecycle of the AI system to physical persons or to existing legal entities? Are there mechanisms in place for a human entity to override decisions made by the AI system? Is there a risk of overreliance on AI systems such that human autonomy is adversely affected or compromised?

Transparency, explainability, accountability, and responsibility: Are users made fully aware when they are interacting with an AI system as opposed to a human being? Are individuals directly or indirectly impacted by the AI system made fully aware of when a decision that impacted them was informed by or made on the basis of an AI system or AI algorithms; the extent to which they are impacted; and the rationale, benefits, and limitations of the decision(s)? Can the AI system make any decisions that the physical persons or legal entities in charge of the system lack expertise or competence to critique, modify, or override?

Awareness and literacy: Is the language used to present the system appropriate for users? If the system will only be used internally, what is the level of competency of those who will interact with it? If the system will be used by the public, can people report their experience interacting with the system and concerns related to its effects? Is the process for doing so simple, accessible, and clearly advertised?

In its recommendations, the UNESCO Global AI Ethics and Governance Observatory (UNESCO, 2023) highlighted concerns that are especially relevant to behavioral health organizations and practitioners:

- The importance of regulating prediction, detection, and treatment solutions for healthcare in AI applications by ensuring oversight to minimize and mitigate bias.
- The inclusion of the professional, the client, or caregiver or service user as a "domain expert" in all relevant steps when developing the algorithms.
- Rigorous attention to privacy because of the potential need for client monitoring.
- Assurance that all relevant national and international data protection requirements are met.
- Having effective mechanisms in place so that those whose personal data are being analyzed are aware of and provide informed consent for the use and analysis of their data without preventing access to care.
- Decisions on final diagnosis and treatment that are always made by humans while acknowledging that AI systems can assist in their work.
- A review of AI systems, where necessary, by an ethical research committee before clinical use.

The UNESCO Global AI Ethics and Governance Observatory (UNESCO, 2023) recommendations focused especially on the ethical implications of organizations' and practitioners' use of social robots to provide care and assistance to clients. The Observatory recommended development of ethics-informed guidelines governing human–robot interactions and their effects on human-to-human relationships. It also highlighted the ethical implications of the use of robots in care for older persons and persons with disabilities and as companions for children and adults. The UNESCO recommendations stated that standards should ensure that human–robot interactions comply with the same values and principles that apply to any other AI systems, including human rights and fundamental freedoms, the promotion of diversity, and the protection of vulnerable people or people in vulnerable situations. Standards should ensure that users can easily identify whether they are interacting with a living being or with an AI system imitating human or animal characteristics and can effectively refuse such interaction and request human intervention.

The International Organization for Standardization (ISO)—an independent, nongovernmental, international standard development organization comprising representatives from the national standards organizations of member countries—is also actively engaged in the development of national and international standards pertaining to the use of AI (ISO, n.d.). These universal standards address ethical concerns that are especially relevant to behavioral healthcare:

Fairness: Datasets used for training the AI system must avoid discrimination.

Transparency: AI systems should be designed in a way that allows users to understand how the algorithms work.

Nonmaleficence: AI systems should avoid harming individuals, society, and the environment.

Accountability: AI developers and policymakers must ensure that AI is used responsibly.

Privacy: AI must protect users' personal data, which involves mechanisms for individuals to control how information about them is collected and used.

Robustness: AI systems should be secure and be designed to prevent adversarial attacks and unexpected inputs.

Inclusiveness: Development of AI systems should draw on diverse perspectives to help identify and address ethical concerns.

ORGANIZATIONAL GUIDELINES FOR EMPLOYEES

Behavioral health organizations should develop ethics-informed guidelines for employees' use of AI. Spisak et al. (2023) argued that state-of-the-art protocols should address the following:

Informed consent: Obtain voluntary and informed agreement from employees to participate in any AI-powered intervention after the employees are provided with all the relevant information about the initiative. This information includes the program's purpose, procedures, and potential risks and benefits.

Aligned interests: Ensure that the goals, risks, and benefits for both the employer and employee are clearly articulated and aligned.

Opt in and easy exits: Employees must opt into AI-powered programs without feeling forced or coerced, and they can easily withdraw from the program at any time without any negative consequences and without explanation.

Conversational transparency: When AI-based conversational agents are used, the sponsoring agent should formally reveal any persuasive objectives the system aims to achieve through dialogue with the employee.

Debiased and explainable AI: Explicitly outline the steps taken to remove, minimize, and mitigate bias in AI-powered employee interventions—especially for disadvantaged and vulnerable groups—and provide transparent explanations about how AI systems arrive at their decisions and actions.

AI training and development: Provide continuous employee training and development to ensure the safe and responsible use of AI-powered tools.

Health and well-being: Identify types of AI-induced stress, discomfort, or harm to users and articulate steps to minimize risks (for example, how the employer will minimize stress caused by constant AI-powered monitoring of employee behavior).

Data collection: Identify what data will be collected, if data collection involves any invasive or intrusive procedures (for example, the use of webcams in remote working situations), and what steps will be taken to minimize risk.

Data sharing: Disclose any intention to share personal data, with whom, and why.

Privacy and security: Articulate protocols for maintaining privacy, storing employee data securely, and what steps will be taken in the event of a privacy breach.

Third-party disclosure: Disclose all third parties used to provide and maintain AI content, what the third party's role is, and how the third party will ensure employee privacy.

Communication: Inform employees about changes in data collection, data management, or data sharing as well as any changes in AI assets or third-party relationships.

Laws and regulations: Express ongoing commitment to comply with all laws and regulations related to employee data and the use of AI.

CONCLUSION

In this chapter, I provided an overview of a range of risk management challenges associated with behavioral health practitioners' use of AI. I discussed the key concept of standard of care and its application to AI. I focused especially on practitioners' and legal experts' evolving understanding of the substantive standard of care related to AI use in behavioral healthcare and the importance of practitioners' implementation of a procedural standard of care when deciding how to use AI. I reviewed the elements of a comprehensive privacy audit and discussed the importance of malpractice insurance to protect practitioners who use AI. I also highlighted guidelines that behavioral health organizations can adopt related to employees' use of AI.

Conclusion

AI IS HERE TO STAY. SOME BEHAVIORAL HEALTH PRACTITIONERS ARE enthused about the benefits of AI; others are skeptical or wary. Whether or not you are an enthusiastic proponent of AI in behavioral health, it is vitally important to have a firm grasp of the myriad ways in which AI is being used in the behavioral health professions, ethical issues that are associated with AI, best practices related to AI use, and practical risk management steps practitioners can take to protect clients and themselves.

Moving forward, behavioral health practitioners must acquaint themselves with evolving ethics-informed standards pertaining to AI, relevant legal guidelines, and opportunities to engage in advocacy to promote the ethical use of AI. Practitioners would do well to monitor national and international efforts to develop and refine ethics-informed standards. In recent years, cutting-edge international collaboration among prominent organizations has identified several key priorities and agenda items that are especially relevant to the behavioral health professions with respect to ethical effects, ethical governance and stewardship, data policy, environment and ecosystems, gender, culture, education and research, and health and social well-being (UNESCO, 2021, 2023).

ETHICAL EFFECTS

Regarding the ethical effects of AI, behavioral health practitioners should seek to do the following:

- Conduct ethical impact assessments to identify and assess benefits, concerns, and risks of AI systems and develop appropriate risk prevention, mitigation, and monitoring measures. Such assessments should pay particular attention to the rights of marginalized and vulnerable people. Ethical impact assessments should be transparent and open to the public. Such assessments should also be multidisciplinary, multistakeholder, multicultural, pluralistic, and inclusive.

- Develop due diligence and oversight mechanisms to identify, prevent, mitigate, and account for how AI affects respect for human rights. AI sponsors should assess the socioeconomic effects of AI systems on poverty and attempt to reduce the digital divide between people living in wealth and poverty.
- Enhance users' decision-making autonomy and reduce any forms of manipulation and coercion.
- Monitor all steps taken to design and implement AI.
- Promote reasonable regulation by licensing boards and other governmental entities to protect AI users from harm. Regulation should establish appropriate oversight mechanisms that enable the assessment of algorithmic fairness and bias.

ETHICAL GOVERNANCE AND STEWARDSHIP

In ethical governance and stewardship AI activities, behavioral health practitioners should seek to do the following:

- Ensure that AI governance mechanisms are inclusive, transparent, multidisciplinary, multilateral, and multistakeholder.
- Ensure that harms caused by AI are investigated vigorously and addressed diligently.
- Carry out transparent self-assessment of existing and proposed AI systems, including the assessment of whether the adoption of AI is appropriate and includes ways to protect human rights.
- Encourage public entities and private sector companies and organizations to involve different stakeholders in their AI governance and consider including an independent AI ethics officer or a comparable mechanism to oversee ethical impact assessment, auditing, and continuous monitoring efforts to ensure compliance with prevailing ethical standards.

- Implement policies to ensure that the actions of AI sponsors are consistent with international human rights law, standards, and principles while taking into consideration relevant cultural and social diversities, including local customs and religious traditions.
- Put in place mechanisms to require AI sponsors to disclose and prevent any kind of stereotyping in the outcomes of AI systems and data. AI protocols should prevent cultural, economic, and social inequalities; prejudice; the spreading of disinformation and misinformation; and disruption of freedom of expression and access to information.
- Implement policies to enhance diversity and inclusiveness in AI development teams and ensure equal access to AI technologies and their benefits, particularly for marginalized groups.
- Develop and implement reasonable regulatory protocols to enhance accountability and responsibility for the content and outcomes of AI systems at the different phases of their lifecycle.
- Set clear requirements for AI system transparency to help ensure trust. Such requirements should involve the design and implementation of mechanisms that take into consideration the nature of AI tools, target audience, and feasibility of each particular AI protocol.

DATA POLICY

In AI data policy, behavioral health practitioners should seek to take these steps:

- Develop data governance strategies that ensure the continual evaluation of the quality of training data for AI systems. These strategies should include ways for developers to learn from and address mistakes.
- Put in place appropriate safeguards to protect users' privacy in accordance with international law, including mechanisms to prevent inappropriate and unauthorized surveillance.
- Ensure that individuals retain rights over their personal data in a way that promotes transparency, appropriate safeguards for the processing of sensitive data, an appropriate level of data protection, effective and meaningful accountability mechanisms, users' ability to access and

erase their personal data in AI systems to the extent permitted by law, and an appropriate level of protection against inappropriate or unauthorized use of AI data for commercial purposes.

- Establish data policies, or reinforce existing ones, to ensure full security for personal and sensitive data, which, if disclosed, may cause damage, injury, or hardship to individuals. Examples include data relating to criminal offenses, proceedings, and convictions; biometric, genetic, and health data; and personal data relating to race, color, descent, gender, age, language, religion, political opinion, national origin, ethnic origin, social origin, economic or social condition of birth, or disability, and any other personal characteristics.

ENVIRONMENT AND ECOSYSTEMS

When considering the effects of AI on the environment and ecosystems, behavioral health practitioners should seek to

- assess the direct and indirect environmental effects of AI, including its carbon footprint, energy consumption, and the environmental effects of raw material extraction to support the manufacturing of AI technologies.
- reduce the environmental effects of AI technologies.
- ensure compliance of all AI sponsors with environmental law.

GENDER

With respect to gender and AI, behavioral health practitioners should seek to

- enhance the use of AI to promote gender equality.
- prevent the use of AI in ways that discriminate based on gender and exacerbate gender gaps.
- ensure that AI does not promote or exacerbate gender stereotyping, discriminatory biases, harassment, bullying, or human trafficking.

CULTURE

With respect to cultural competence, humility, and education in AI, behavioral health practitioners should seek to do the following:

- Use AI to preserve, enrich, understand, and promote cultural heritage, including endangered and Indigenous languages, for example by introducing or updating educational programs related to the application of AI systems in diverse cultural contexts and by ensuring diverse participation in their development.
- Examine and address the cultural effect of AI systems, especially natural language processing applications, such as automated translation and voice assistants, on the nuances of human language and expression. Such assessments should provide input for the design and implementation of strategies that maximize the benefits of these systems by bridging cultural gaps and increasing human understanding as well as addressing the ways in which AI could lead to the disappearance of endangered languages, local dialects, and tonal and cultural variations associated with human language and expression.

EDUCATION AND RESEARCH

In education and research, behavioral health practitioners should seek to

- invest in and promote digital, media, and information literacy skills to strengthen critical thinking and competencies needed to understand the use and implication of AI to mitigate and counter disinformation, misinformation, and hate speech.
- promote understanding and evaluation of both the positive and potentially harmful effects of AI.

HEALTH AND SOCIAL WELL-BEING

When considering health and social well-being, behavioral health practitioners should seek to take these measures:

- Ensure that the development and implementation of AI related to behavioral healthcare are regulated so that they are safe, effective, efficient, and evidence based. AI sponsors should actively involve clients and their representatives in all relevant steps of the development of the system.

- Focus on regulating behavioral health prediction, detection, and treatment using AI applications by
    - ensuring oversight to minimize and mitigate algorithmic bias.
    - ensuring that the professional, client, caregiver, or service user is included as a "domain expert" in the team in all relevant steps when developing the algorithms.
    - paying attention to privacy because of the potential need for monitoring of clients' behavioral health status, ensuring that all relevant national and international data protection requirements are met.
    - ensuring effective mechanisms so that AI users whose personal data are being analyzed are aware of and provide informed consent for the use and analysis of their data without preventing AI users' access to health and behavioral healthcare.
    - ensuring that humans make decisions on behavioral healthcare as well as final decisions about diagnosis and treatment with the acknowledgment that AI systems can also assist in their work.
    - ensuring, where necessary, the review of AI systems by an ethics research committee before clinical use.
- Promote research on the effects and regulation of potential harms to mental health related to AI use, including, among other risks and challenges, higher degrees of depression, anxiety, social isolation, addiction, trafficking, radicalization, and misinformation.

Who among us could have imagined at the start of our careers that AI would be prominent in behavioral healthcare? Perhaps none of us. But here we are. How AI will shape the behavioral health professions is hard to forecast. As with any cutting-edge innovation, it will take time to fully identify and understand potential and actual benefits and challenges, formulate sound ethics guidelines, and create constructive risk management protocols. At the very least, behavioral health practitioners must be active participants in these ongoing efforts and dialogues. That is at the center of what ethical practice requires.

References

Abd-alrazaq, A., Alhuwail, D., Schneider, J., Toro, C. T., Ahmed, A., Alzubaidi, M., Alajlani, M., & Househ, M. (2022). The performance of artificial intelligence-driven technologies in diagnosing mental disorders: An umbrella review. *npj Digital Medicine, 5,* Article 87. https://www.nature.com/articles/s41746-022-00631-8

Adler, S. (2017, March 7). Updated HIPAA compliance audit toolkit issued by AHIMA. *HIPAA Journal.* https://www.hipaajournal.com/hipaa-compliance-audit-toolkit-issued-by-ahima-8719/

Allegheny County Department of Human Services. (2016). *Allegheny Family Screening Tool.* Allegheny County. https://www.alleghenycounty.us/Services/Human-Services-DHS/DHS-News-and-Events/Accomplishments-and-Innovations/Allegheny-Family-Screening-Tool

American Association for Marriage and Family Therapy. (2015). *Code of ethics.* https://www.aamft.org/AAMFT/Legal_Ethics/Code_of_Ethics.aspx

American Counseling Association. (2014). *ACA code of ethics.* https://www.counseling.org/docs/default-source/ethics/2014-aca-code-of-ethics.pdf

American Psychological Association. (2017). *Ethical principles of psychologists and code of conduct* (2002, amended effective June 1, 2010, and January 1, 2017). https://www.apa.org/ethics/code

Asakura, K., Occhiuto, K., Todd, S., Leithead, C., & Clapperton, R. (2020). A call to action on artificial intelligence and social work education: Lessons learned from a simulation project using natural language processing. *Journal of Teaching in Social Work, 40,* 501–518. https://doi.org/10.1080/08841233.2020.1813234

Ashok, M., Madan, R., Joha, A., & Sivarajah, U. (2022). Ethical framework for artificial intelligence and digital technologies. *International Journal of Information Management, 62,* Article 102433. https://doi.org/10.1016/j.ijinfomgt.2021.102433

Ballantyne, N. (2023, August 6). *The harm that data do: The case of the Allegheny Family Screening Tool.* Medium. https://medium.com/@neilballantyne/the-harm-that-data-do-the-case-of-the-allegheny-family-screening-tool-5f9fca22e0b2

Bankins, S., & Formosa, P. (2023). The ethical implications of artificial intelligence (AI) for meaningful work. *Journal of Business Ethics, 185*, 725–740. https://doi.org/10.1007/s10551-023-05339-7

Barsky, A. E. (2019). *Ethics and values in social work: An integrated approach for a comprehensive curriculum* (2nd ed.). Oxford University Press.

Barsky, A. E. (2024). *Clinicians in court: A guide to subpoenas, depositions, testifying, and everything else you need to know* (3rd ed.). Guilford Press.

Bateman, K. (2021, December 22). *4 ways artificial intelligence is improving mental health therapy.* World Economic Forum. https://www.weforum.org/agenda/2021/12/ai-mental-health-cbt-therapy/

Beauchamp, T. L., & Childress, J. F. (1979). *Principles of biomedical ethics.* Oxford University Press.

Beauchamp, T. L., & Childress, J. F. (2019). *Principles of biomedical ethics* (8th ed.). Oxford University Press.

Berg, J. W., Appelbaum, P. S., Lidz, C. W., & Parker, L. S. (2001). *Informed consent: Legal theory and clinical practice* (2nd ed.). Oxford University Press.

Carroll, M. (2023, December 5). *AI tool could increase the number of people exiting homelessness, reduce racial bias in services: Report.* Phys.org. https://phys.org/news/2023-12-ai-tool-people-exiting-homelessness.html#google_vignette

Carter, P. I. (2025). *HIPAA compliance handbook 2025.* Wolters Kluwer.

Char, D. S., Abràmoff, M. D., & Feudtner, C. (2020). Identifying ethical considerations for machine learning healthcare applications. *American Journal of Bioethics, 20*, 7–17. https://doi.org/10.1080/15265161.2020.1819469

Chen, I. Y., Pierson, E., Rose, S., Joshi, S., Ferryman, K., & Ghassemi, M. (2021). Ethical machine learning in healthcare. *Annual Review of Biomedical Data Science, 4*, 123–144. https://doi.org/10.1146/annurev-biodatasci-092820-114757

Copeland, B. J. (n.d.). *Artificial intelligence.* Britannica. Retrieved October 4, 2024, from https://www.britannica.com/technology/artificial-intelligence

Diez, E. R. (2023). Artificial intelligence and social work: Contributions to an ethical artificial intelligence at the service of the people. In A. López Peláez & G. Kirwan (Eds.), *The Routledge international handbook of digital social work* (pp. 368–381). Routledge.

Dilorenzo, P. S. (2023, July 6). *Child welfare should go slow on AI.* The Imprint: Youth & Family News. https://imprintnews.org/opinion/child-welfare-should-go-slow-ai/242819

Dunleavy, B. P. (2021, October 15). *Study: AI can help diagnose mental health disorders where access to care lacking.* UPI. https://www.upi.com/Science_News/2021/10/15/AI-machine-learning-mental-health-diagnosis-study/8781634316118/

Formosa, P. (2021). Robot autonomy vs. human anatomy: Social robots, artificial intelligence (AI), and the nature of autonomy. *Minds and Machines, 31*, 595–616. https://doi.org/10.1007/s11023-021-09579-2

Gattadahalli, S. (2020, November 3). Ten steps to ethics-based governance of AI in health care. *STAT.* https://www.statnews.com/2020/11/03/artificial-intelligence-health-care-ten-steps-to-ethics-based-governance/

Giarmoleo, F. V., Ferrero, I., Rocchi, M., & Pellegrini, M. M. (2023). What ethics can say on artificial intelligence: Insights from a systematic literature review. *Business and Society Review, 129*, 258–292. https://doi.org/10.1111/basr.12336

Gillingham, P. (2019). Can predictive algorithms assist decision-making in social work with children and families? *Child Abuse Review, 28*, 114–126. https://doi.org/10.1002/car.2547

Goldkind, L. (2021). Social work and artificial intelligence: Into the matrix [Commentary]. *Social Work, 66*, 372–374. https://doi.org/10.1093/sw/swab028

Gonzales, M. (2023, October 6). How AI brings the human element to SUD treatment while saving time. *Addiction Treatment Business.* https://bhbusiness.com/2023/10/06/how-ai-brings-the-human-element-to-sud-treatment-while-saving-time/

Grote, T., & Berens, P. (2020). On the ethics of algorithmic decision-making in healthcare. *Journal of Medical Ethics, 46*, 205–211. https://doi.org/10.1136/medethics-2019-105586

Grządzielewska, M. (2021). Using machine learning in burnout prediction: A survey. *Child and Adolescent Social Work Journal, 38*, 175–180. https://doi.org/10.1007/s10560-020-00733-w

Hagendorff, T. (2020). The ethics of AI ethics: An evaluation of guidelines. *Minds and Machines, 30*, 99–120. https:/doi.org/10.1007/s11023-020-09517-8

Health Insurance Portability and Accountability Act of 1996, 42 U.S.C. § 1320d-6 (1996). https://www.hhs.gov/hipaa/for-professionals/privacy/laws-regulations/index.html

International Organization for Standardization. (n.d.). *Building a responsible AI: How to manage the AI ethics debate.* ISO. https://www.iso.org/artificial-intelligence/responsible-ai-ethics

Jacobi, C. B., & Christensen, M. (2023). Functions, utilities, and limitations: A scoping study of decision support algorithms in social work. *Journal of*

Evidence-Based Social Work, *20*, 323–341. https://doi.org/10.1080/26408066.2022.2159777

Johnson, S. L. J. (2019). AI, machine learning, and ethics in health care. *Journal of Legal Medicine*, *39*, 427–441. https://doi.org/10.1080/01947648.2019.1690604

Keddell, E. (2019). Algorithmic justice in child protection: Statistical fairness, social justice and the implications for practice. *Social Sciences*, *8*, Article 281. https://doi.org/10.3390/socsci8100281

Keegan, J. M. (2023, May 23). ChatGPT is a plagiarism machine: So why do administrators have their heads in the sand? [Opinion]. *Chronicle of Higher Education*. https://www.chronicle.com/article/chatgpt-is-a-plagiarism-machine?cid=gen_sign_in

Lanier, P., Rodriguez, M., Verbiest, S., Bryant, K., Guan, T., & Zolotor, A. (2020). Preventing infant maltreatment with predictive analytics: Applying ethical principles to evidence-based child welfare policy. *Journal of Family Violence*, *35*, 1–13. https://doi.org/10.1007/s10896-019-00074-y

Lee, N., Resnick, P., & Barton, G. (2019, May 22). *Algorithmic bias detection and mitigation: Best practices and policies to reduce consumer harms*. Brookings. https://www.brookings.edu/articles/algorithmic-bias-detection-and-mitigation-best-practices-and-policies-to-reduce-consumer-harms/

Li, F., Ruijs, N., & Lu, Y. (2023). Ethics & AI: A systematic review on ethical concerns and related strategies for designing with AI in healthcare. *AI*, *4*, 28–53. https://doi.org/10.3390/ai4010003

Liedgren, P., Elvhage, G., Ehrenberg, A., & Kullberg, C. (2016). The use of decision support systems in social work: A scoping study literature review. *Journal of Evidence-Informed Social Work*, *13*, 1–20. https://doi.org/10.1080/15433714.2014.914992

LII Legal Information Institute. (n.d.). *Jaffe v. Redmond (95-266), 518 U.S. 1 (1996)*. https://www.law.cornell.edu/supct/html/95-266.ZO.html

Lu, S. (2023, October 23). *Can AI learn the language of addiction?* National Institute on Drug Abuse. https://nida.nih.gov/news-events/nida-asks/can-ai-learn-language-addiction

Luxton, D. D. (Ed.). (2016). *Artificial intelligence in behavioral and mental health care*. Elsevier Academic Press.

Martin, K. (2019). Designing ethical algorithms. *MIS Quarterly Executive*, *18*, Article 5. https://doi.org/10.17705/2msqe.00012

Molala, T. S., & Mbaya, T. W. (2023). Social work and artificial intelligence: Towards the electronic social work field of specialisation. *International Journal of Social Science Research and Review*, *6*, 613–621. https://doi.org/10.47814/ijssrr.v6i4.1206

Morley, J., Machado, C. C. V., Burr, C., Cowls, J., Joshi, I., Taddeo, M., & Floridi, L. (2020). The ethics of AI in health care: A mapping review. *Social Science & Medicine, 260*, Article 113172. https://doi.org/10.1016/j.socscimed.2020.113172

Murphy, K., Di Ruggiero, E., Upshur, R., Willison, D. J., Malhotra, N., Cai, J. C., Malhotra, N., Lui, V., & Gibson, J. (2021). Artificial intelligence for good health: A scoping review of the ethics literature. *BMC Medical Ethics, 22*, Article 14. https://doi.org/10.1186/s12910-021-00577-8

NAADAC. (2021). *Code of ethics.* https://www.naadac.org/assets/2416/naadac_code_of_ethics_112021.pdf

National Association of Social Workers. (n.d.). *8 ethical considerations for the use of artificial intelligence in social work.* Retrieved November 15, 2024, from https://www.socialworkers.org/About/Ethics/Ethics-Education-and-Resources/Ethics-8/8-Ethical-Considerations-for-the-Use-of-Artificial-Intelligence-in-Social-Work

National Association of Social Workers. (2021). *Code of ethics of the National Association of Social Workers.* https://www.socialworkers.org/About/Ethics/Code-of-Ethics

National Association of Social Workers, Association of Social Work Boards, Council on Social Work Education, & Clinical Social Work Association. (2017). *NASW, ASWB, CSWE, & CSWA standards for technology in social work practice.* https://www.socialworkers.org/Practice/NASW-Practice-Standards-Guidelines/Standards-for-Technology-in-Social-Work-Practice

National Institute of Standards and Technology. (2024, April). *Artificial intelligence risk management framework: Generative artificial intelligence profile* (Report No. NIST AI 600-1). U.S. Department of Commerce. https://airc.nist.gov/docs/NIST.AI.600-1.GenAI-Profile.ipd.pdf

Orr, W., & Davis, J. L. (2020). Attributions of ethical responsibility by artificial intelligence practitioners. *Information, Communication & Society, 23*, 719–735. https://doi.org/10.1080/1369118X.2020.1713842

Pascoe, K. M. (2023). Considerations for integrating technology into social work practice: A content analysis of nine social work associations' codes of ethics. *International Social Work, 66*, 298–312. https://doi.org/10.1177/0020872820980833

Petrosyan, L. (2024, August 18). *Introduction to artificial intelligence.* National Fair Housing Alliance: Responsible AI Lab. https://rail.nationalfairhousing.org/2024/08/18/introduction-to-artificial-intelligence/

Plante, T. G. (2023, February 6). *The ethics of AI applications for mental health care.* Markkula Center for Applied Ethics at Santa Clara University. https://www

.scu.edu/ethics-spotlight/generative-ai-ethics/the-ethics-of-ai-applications-for-mental-health-care/

Plato. (1994–2000). *Laws* (B. Jowett, Trans.). The Internet Classics Archive: https://classics.mit.edu/Plato/laws.html (Original work published ca. 360 B.C.E.)

Pocock, K. (2024, March 28). Is ChatGPT plagiarism free? *PC Guide.* https://www.pcguide.com/apps/is-chat-gpt-plagiarism-free/

Rasure, E. (2021, July 19). *Gamification: What it is, how it works, risks.* Investopedia. https://www.investopedia.com/terms/g/gamification.asp

Reamer, F. G. (2021). *Ethics & risk management in online & distance behavioral health.* Cognella.

Reamer, F. G. (2023a). Artificial intelligence in social work: Emerging ethical issues. *International Journal of Social Work Values and Ethics, 20,* 52–71.

Reamer, F. G. (2023b). Ethical practice in a post-*Roe* world: A guide for social workers. *Social Work, 68,* 150–158. https://doi.org/10.1093/sw/swad004

Reamer, F. G. (2023c). *Ethical standards in social work: A review of the NASW Code of Ethics* (rev. 3rd ed.). NASW Press.

Reamer, F. G. (2023d). *Risk management in the behavioral health professions: A practical guide to preventing malpractice and licensing-board complaints.* Columbia University Press.

Reamer, F. G. (2024). *Social work values and ethics* (6th ed.). Columbia University Press.

Rice, E., Milburn, N., Vayanos, P., Rountree, J., Hill, C., Petering, R., Blackwell, B., Santillano, R., Onasch-Vera, L., Winetrobe Nadel, H., Tang, B., Aghaei, S., Hsu, H.-T., & Petry, L. (2023). *CESTTRR: Coordinated entry system triage tool research and refinement.* USC Center for AI in Society. https://cais.usc.edu/wp-content/uploads/2023/11/CESTTRR-Final-Report-2023.pdf

Rice, E., Yoshioka-Maxwell, A., Petering, R., Onasch-Vera, L., Craddock, J., Tambe, M., Yadav, A., Wilder, B., Woo, D., Winetrobe, H., & Wilson, N. (2018). Piloting the use of artificial intelligence to enhance HIV prevention interventions for youth experiencing homelessness. *Journal of the Society for Social Work and Research, 9,* 551–573. https://doi.org/10.1086/701439

Robinson, N. L., & Kavanagh, D. J. (2021). A social robot to deliver a psychotherapeutic treatment: Qualitative responses by participants in a randomized controlled trial and future design recommendations. *International Journal of Human-Computer Studies, 155,* Article 102700. https://doi.org/10.1016/j.ijhcs.2021.102700

Rogers, M. (2024). *AI enabled community supervision for criminal justice services.* U.S. Department of Justice, Office of Justice Programs. https://www.ojp.gov/pdffiles1/nij/grants/308693.pdf

Romm, E. L., & Tsigelny, I. F. (2020). Artificial intelligence in drug treatment. *Annual Review of Pharmacology and Toxicology*, *60*, 353–369. https://doi.org/10.1146/annurev-pharmtox-010919-023746

Rong, G., Mendez, A., Bou Assi, E., Zhao, B., & Sawan, M. (2020). Artificial intelligence in healthcare: Review and prediction case studies. *Engineering*, *6*, 291–301. https://doi.org/10.1016/j.eng.2019.08.015

Royer, A. (2021, October 14). *The wellness industry's risky embrace of AI-driven mental health care*. Brookings. https://www.brookings.edu/articles/the-wellness-industrys-risky-embrace-of-ai-driven-mental-health-care/

Rubeis, G. (2022). iHealth: The ethics of artificial intelligence and big data in mental healthcare. *Internet Interventions*, *28*, Article 100518. https://doi.org/10.1016/j.invent.2022.100518

Russo, J., Woods, D., Drake, G. B., Jackson, B. A. (2019, October 28). *Leveraging technology to enhance community supervision: Identifying needs to address current and emerging concerns.* RAND Corporation. https://www.rand.org/pubs/research_reports/RR3213.html

Sarraf, S. (2021, November 29). *UNESCO launches global standard for AI ethics.* InfoWorld. https://www.infoworld.com/article/3642831/unesco-launches-global-standard-for-ai-ethics.html

Schneider, D., & Seelmeyer, U. (2019). Challenges in using big data to develop decision support systems for social work in Germany. *Journal of Technology in Human Services*, *37*, 113–128. https://doi.org/10.1080/15228835.2019.1614513

Schreiber, M. (2024, March 25). *Why large language models like ChatGPT treat Black- and White-sounding names differently.* Stanford University, Human-Centered Artificial Intelligence. https://hai.stanford.edu/news/why-large-language-models-chatgpt-treat-black-and-white-sounding-names-differently

Seniutis, M., Gružauskas, V., Lileikiene, A., & Navickas, V. (2024). Conceptual framework for ethical artificial intelligence development in social services sector. *Human Technology*, *20*, 6–24. https://doi.org/10.14254/1795-6889.2024.20-1.1

Søbjerg, L. M. (2022). Developing a statistical model for assessment of referrals of children at risk. *Child Abuse Review*, *31*, Article e2749. https://doi.org/10.1002/car.2749

Spisak, B., Rosenberg, L. B., & Beilby, M. (2023, June 30). 13 principles for using AI responsibly. *Harvard Business Review.* https://hbr.org/2023/06/13-principles-for-using-ai-responsibly

Tambe, M., & Rice, E. (Eds.). (2018). *Artificial intelligence and social work.* Cambridge University Press.

Terra, M., Baklola, M., Ali, S., & El-Bastawisy, K. (2023). Opportunities, applications, challenges and ethical implications of artificial intelligence in psychiatry: A narrative review. *Egyptian Journal of Neurology, Psychiatry and Neurosurgery, 59*, Article 80. https://doi.org/10.1186/s41983-023-00681-z

Trail, M. (2024, February 6). *Algorithmic decision-making in child welfare cases and its legal and ethical challenges.* American Bar Association. https://www.americanbar.org/groups/litigation/resources/newsletters/childrens-rights/winter2024-algorithmic-decision-making-in-child-welfare-cases/

Trevor News. (2024, March 4). *The Trevor Project launches new AI tool to support crisis counselor training.* The Trevor Project. https://www.thetrevorproject.org/blog/the-trevor-project-launches-new-ai-tool-to-support-crisis-counselor-training/

United Nations Educational, Scientific and Cultural Organization. (2021, November 23). *Recommendation on the ethics of artificial intelligence.* https://unesdoc.unesco.org/ark:/48223/pf0000381137

United Nations Educational, Scientific and Cultural Organization. (2023). *Ethical impact assessment: A tool of the recommendation on the ethics of artificial intelligence.* https://unesdoc.unesco.org/ark:/48223/pf0000386276/PDF/386276eng.pdf.multi

University of California–Berkeley School of Information. (2020, June 26). *What is machine learning (ML)?* https://ischoolonline.berkeley.edu/blog/what-is-machine-learning/

Wangmo, T., Lipps, M., Kressig, R. W., & Ienca, M. (2019). Ethical concerns with the use of intelligent assistive technology: Findings from a qualitative study with professional stakeholders. *BMC Medical Ethics, 20*, Article 98. https://doi.org/10.1186/s12910-019-0437-z

The White House. (2023, October 30). *President Biden issues executive order on safe, secure, and trustworthy artificial intelligence* [Fact sheet]. https://www.whitehouse.gov/briefing-room/statements-releases/2023/10/30/fact-sheet-president-biden-issues-executive-order-on-safe-secure-and-trustworthy-artificial-intelligence/

Yan, W.-J., Ruan, Q.-N., & Jiang, K. (2023). Challenges of artificial intelligence in recognizing mental disorders. *Diagnostics, 13*, Article 2. https://doi.org/10.3390/diagnostics13010002

Yeazell, S. C., Schwartz, J. C., & Carroll, M. (2022). *Federal rules of civil procedure: With selected statutes, cases, and other materials.* Aspen Publishers.

Index

About the Author

Frederic G. Reamer, PhD, is professor emeritus in the graduate program of the School of Social Work, Rhode Island College. His research and teaching have addressed a wide range of human services issues, including mental health, healthcare, criminal justice, public welfare, and professional ethics. Reamer has served as a social worker in correctional and mental health settings and has lectured extensively nationally and internationally on the subjects of professional ethics and professional malpractice and liability. Reamer received the Distinguished Contributions to Social Work Education Award from the Council on Social Work Education (CSWE; 1995), the Presidential Award from National Association of Social Workers (NASW; 1997), the International Rhoda G. Sarnat Award from NASW (2012), and the Excellence in Ethics Award from NASW (2015). In 2016, NASW named Reamer a Social Work Pioneer. In 2023, he received the Mit Joyner Presidential Award from NASW.

Reamer's books include *The Social Work Ethics Casebook: Cases and Commentary* (revised 2nd edition; NASW Press); *Risk Management in the Behavioral Health Professions: A Practical Guide to Preventing Malpractice and Licensing-Board Complaints* (Columbia University Press); *Risk Management in Social Work: Preventing Professional Malpractice, Liability, and Disciplinary Action* (Columbia University Press); *Heinous Crime: Cases, Causes, and Consequences* (Columbia University Press); *On the Parole Board: Reflections on Crime, Punishment, Redemption, and Justice* (Columbia University Press); *A Guide to Essential Human Services* (NASW Press); *Moral Distress and Injury in Human Services: Cases, Causes, and Strategies for Prevention* (NASW Press); *Criminal Lessons: Case Studies and Commentary on Crime and Justice* (Columbia University Press); *Social Work Values and Ethics* (Columbia University Press); *Boundary Issues and Dual Relationships in the Human Services* (Columbia University

Press); *Ethical Standards in Social Work: A Review of the NASW Code of Ethics* (revised 3rd edition; NASW Press); *The Social Work Ethics Audit: A Risk Management Tool* (NASW Press); *Teens in Crisis: How the Industry Serving Struggling Teens Helps and Hurts Our Kids* (Columbia University Press; with Deborah H. Siegel); *Finding Help for Struggling Teens: A Guide for Parents and the Professionals Who Work with Them* (NASW Press; with Deborah H. Siegel); *Ethics Education in Social Work* (CSWE); *The Foundations of Social Work Knowledge* (Columbia University Press; editor and contributor); *Ethics & Risk Management in Online & Distance Behavioral Health* (Cognella); *Social Work Research and Evaluation Skills: A Case-Based, User-Friendly Approach* (Columbia University Press); *The Philosophical Foundations of Social Work* (Columbia University Press); *AIDS & Ethics* (Columbia University Press; editor and contributor); *Ethical Dilemmas in Social Service* (Columbia University Press); *Rehabilitating Juvenile Justice* (Columbia University Press; coauthor, Charles H. Shireman); and *The Teaching of Social Work Ethics* (The Hastings Center; coauthor, Marcia Abramson). Reamer serves frequently as an expert witness in litigation and licensing-board cases throughout the United States.